A HANDBOOK
TO THE PALACE OF MINOS
AT KNOSSOS

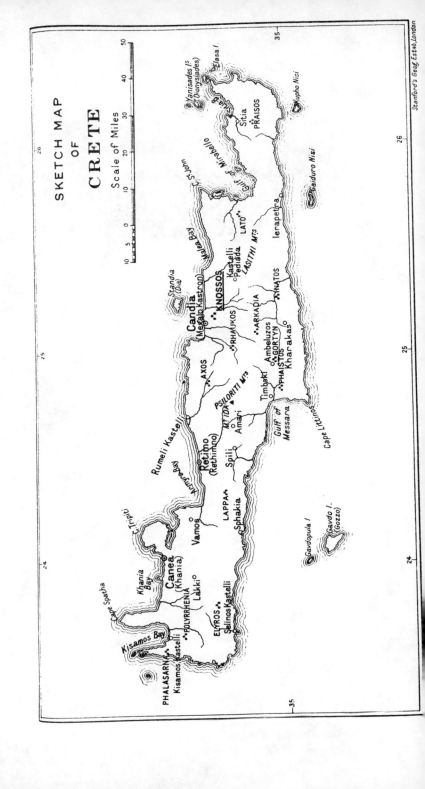

SKETCH MAP
OF
CRETE

Scale of Miles

Stanford's Geog. Estab., London.

A HANDBOOK
TO THE PALACE OF MINOS
AT KNOSSOS

By

J.D.S. PENDLEBURY

INTRODUCTION TO THE AMERICAN EDITION
AND BIBLIOGRAPHY

By

LESLIE PRESTON DAY

ARES PUBLISHERS, INC.
CHICAGO   MCMLXXIX

©1979
NEW MATERIAL
ARES PUBLISHERS INC.
612 N. Michigan Ave., Suite 216
Chicago, Illinois 60611
Printed in the United States of America
International Standard Book Number
0-89005-312-X
81-1365

CONTENTS

INTRODUCTION

Since Pendlebury's *Handbook to the Palace of Minos at Knossos* first appeared in 1933, archaeologists have uncovered a great deal of material and scholars have generated a large amount of information about Minoan civilization. Although Myres and Forsdyke made an excellent synthesis of the then recent material in their 1954 introduction to the *Handbook*, the archaeological discoveries of the last 25 years have increased our knowledge of the culture and history of Minoan Crete even farther. Numerous new guides to the palace at Knossos and handbooks to Minoan civilization have been published, yet Pendlebury's *Handbook* still has great value and charm. Pendlebury knew Knossos better than anyone except Sir Arthur Evans and Duncan Mackenzie, its excavators, and his guide continues to provide the student or visitor with a clear and literate introduction to the site. For this reason it has seemed useful to reprint this book, with a new introduction which summarizes the discoveries of the last 25 years and the recent controversies about Knossos and Minoan culture. For those who wish to know something about these matters beyond the scope of this summary, a bibliography of basic books on Crete and books and articles on important discoveries at Knossos has been included at the end.

In this discussion I will follow the relative dating system which Evans originated based on the pottery sequence at Knossos. His successors elaborated upon this system, but it has met with criticism. Although it nicely divides Minoan history into Early, Middle, and Late phases and subdivides the larger periods into I, II, and III, the terms can be misleading; most importantly, the major divisions (EM, MM, LM) do not correspond to the important architectural stages of the palaces. A further confusion is created by the fact that many of the pottery styles distinguished by Evans are purely palatial in character and were never in use in the smaller towns and villages throughout Crete; MM IIA, for example, seems to have been produced in the palace centers at a time when MM IB pottery was still in use in the rest of the island. Because of these problems, a number of scholars have adopted Platon's dating system, in which the chronological divisions have been based on the building phases of the palaces, rather than on pottery; pre-palatial (EM), proto-palatial (MM I-II), neo-palatial (MM III-LM II), and post-palatial (LM III). While less cumbersome and sometimes less confusing, the scheme suffers from a lack of precision, and Evans' system of pottery dates is still the most accurate.

The absolute dating of these pottery periods has been modified since Pendlebury's time. Advances in scientific dating techniques, particularly the use of radiocarbon dating, have yielded more accurate dates for the earlier periods of Minoan history. Correlations with Egypt still provide the basis for the MM and LM dates, and the dating of Egyptian history has also undergone modification. The following system of absolute dates will be employed here:

EM	I	3000-2600
EM	II	2600-2200
EM	III	2200-2050
MM	I	2050-1800
MM	II	1800-1700
MM	III	1700-1580
LM	IA	1580-1500
LM	IB	1500-1450
LM	II	1450-1400
LM	IIIA:1	1400-1375
LM	IIIA:2	1375-1300
LM	IIIB	1300-1200
LM	IIIC	1200-1050

The British excavation of the Neolithic mound on which the later palace of Knossos was constructed has increased our understanding of the earliest periods of human habitation on Crete (Evans, 1964a, 1964b; Evans et.al. 1968). Beneath the central court at Knossos ten layers of Neolithic settlement were defined, all containing substantial architectural remains. A Carbon 14 sample from the lowest stratum yielded an absolute date of 6341 ± 180 (based on a half life of 5730, not corrected by tree-ring chronology, Cadogan 1976, p. 16) for the

Early Neolithic. Other scattered remains have been found on the island, particularly at Katsamba near Knossos (Alexiou 1954), but Knossos seems to have been the major settlement on Crete in the Neolithic period. There is no new evidence for determining the origins of these Neolithic people. Defining the transition from Neolithic to Early Minoan is still a difficulty, although Renfrew (1972) has tried to clarify the situation by describing a transitional stage, which he calls "Final Neolithic."

The Early Minoan period itself has been the subject of controversy. On the basis of his findings from Phaistos, Levi has questioned the validity of the sequence of phases set up by Evans (Levi 1960, 1964). He has suggested that EM did not exist as a general chronological unit, but was a local phenomenon, since no extensive EM remains have been found stratified between the long Neolithic and Middle Minoan sequences on any palace site. While this theory cannot be disproved, it creates more difficulties than it solves. It seems clear that the builders of the MM palaces removed substantial EM and Late Neolithic layers when levelling those sites, and there is a sufficient number of closed EM deposits from elsewhere in Crete to substantiate the existence of a long EM period. Excavations at Knossos (Hood 1963; Evans 1972) and Lebena (Alexiou 1958, 1960, 1963) have helped to define the pottery sequence of EM I and III, and Warren's dig at the village of Fournou Korifi at Myrtos has provided new information about the nature of settlements of the EM II period (Warren, 1972). Taken with the remains from beneath the West Court at Knossos and those from Vasiliki, the Myrtos material indicates a sophisticated EM II period, apparently with a tradition of large architectural complexes which may have inspired the later palaces. In the Early Minoan period the center of Minoan civilization seems to have shifted from Knossos to the East and South of the island, though Knossos has been shown by recent excavations to have been more important than was previously thought.

The Middle Minoan I period was marked by the building of the palaces at Knossos, Phaistos, and Mallia. Evans assigned their construction to the beginning of the period, but Levi has found nothing earlier than MM IB at Phaistos, and many scholars have now accepted MM IB as the beginning of the palatial age. Continuing stratigraphic excavations at Knossos have helped to refine the MM I-II ceramic sequence, although not much more is known now about the architectural features of the early palace than Pendlebury knew. At Phaistos, however, Levi has uncovered substantial remains of the MM I-II palace South and West of the West Court of the later palace, which was untouched by later rebuilding. He has distinguished three strata, all separated by thick layers of concrete, the last of which he dated to MM IIIB. This contradicts the situation at Knossos, where the second palace was built in MM IIIA, and other scholars have reinterpreted Levi's evidence to bring the Phaistos sequence into line with that at Knossos (Walberg, 1976). At Mallia, although many remains of the MM I-II period have come to light in the surrounding areas, there is little information about the early palace itself.

After major damage by earthquake at the end of MM II, the palaces at Knossos, Phaistos, and Mallia were rebuilt on an even grander scale, while at the eastern tip of the island a new palace was erected at Kato Zakro. At Knossos, the excavations of the Royal Road (Hood 1963) have clarified the MM III-LM II pottery sequence, and Popham has uncovered a large LM house next to the Little Palace, which Evans had labelled the "Unexplored Mansion" (Popham 1973). Little new exploration has been done in the palace proper, although Graham's architectural studies have revealed some of the underlying principles on which the palaces were constructed (Graham 1962). He has identified the basic Minoan unit of measure (11 15/16 ft.), and he has demonstrated the similarity of the residential quarter, *piano nobile*, and banquet hall at Knossos to those in the other palaces. On the basis of the support walls in the West Magazines and on analogy with the other palaces he has shown that the *piano nobile* at Knossos could not have been as Evans reconstructed it (p. 38), but should have three large rooms over the West Magazines. He has also suggested that the North Pillar Hall supported a large Banquet Hall, similar to ones in the other palaces, particularly Mallia.

At Mallia the areas around the palace have been extensively excavated. In addition to many private houses, the French excavators have cleared the area North of the palace, which included a large open space or "agora" surrounded by buildings (van Effenterre 1969). The excavators interpret this as an indication of a major political development, representing an erosion of the absolute power of the Minoan monarch. Other interpretations are possible; Graham (Graham n.d.) thinks it may have been a practise ring for bull-leaping. Investigations at Mallia, Knossos, and Zakro have shown that these palaces also were surrounded by extensive settlements.

The newly discovered palace at Kato Zakro, uncovered in the 1960's, was not thoroughly looted, and it has yielded vast quantities of objects stored in the palace at the time of its destruction. Although smaller than the other palaces, it conforms to the same basic scheme. Peculiarities include its elaborate water supply and a series of rooms, possibly for ritual banqueting, along the West side of the Central Court. Other excavations have investigated non-palatial sites on Crete; of particular interest is a new Minoan villa excavated by Cadogan at Pyrgos, Myrtos (Cadogan 1976).

Considerable archaeological activity in the islands of the Aegean has increased our knowledge of Cretan civilization and its relationship with its neighbors. The excavations of Ayia Irini on Keos, Akrotiri on Thera, Phylakopi on Melos, and Kastri on Kythera have revealed settlements with strong Minoan connections. Though much evidence exists for the cultural influence of Crete on these islands, and possible economic connections as well, nothing has been discovered which shows that they were Minoan colonies or under the political domination of a "Minoan Thalassocracy." These island sites, along with all the Cretan sites except Knossos, were destroyed at the end of LM IB, c. 1450 B.C.

Perhaps no subject has engendered so much scholarly debate as the destruction of Minoan civilization. Controversy has centered around two quite separate problems; why and how did Cretan sites fall, and when was Knossos itself destroyed. The sequence of events has been clarified since Pendlebury's time. All other Minoan sites were destroyed at the end of LM IB, and in most cases there are traces of burning. Knossos, however, continued without a break into the succeeding LM II period. There are signs of a new population in this period: pottery styles reminiscent of mainland ceramics, a change in burial customs to interment in Chamber tombs, new and superior weapons buried with the dead, and a different language represented in the Linear B tablets (Hood 1952). Linear B has been deciphered to the agreement of most scholars. Though the writing system is the same as the earlier Cretan Linear A script, the language represents an early form of Greek. The conclusion seems inescapable that Knossos was under the control of Mainland Greeks in LM II. Many theories have been propounded about the reasons for the fall of Crete. In light of the apparent occupation of Knossos by Mycenaeans in LM II, an obvious explanation is that Crete collapsed as a result of military conquest by people from the Mainland. Such a theory is attractive, particularly with reference to the aggressive nature of the Mycenaeans and their immediate absorption of Minoan trade routes. The idea does not, however, explain the wide scale of the destructions and their violence, not only on Crete, but also on the islands. There is no evidence for hostility between Crete and the Mainland before LM IB, but rather the Greeks seem to have been captivated by Minoan culture.

Recently, more popular theories have connected the collapse of Minoan civilization with the eruption of the volcano on Thera (Santorini), known to have occurred around this time. The destruction of Cretan sites could have been connected with the ensuing tidal wave, the fall of volcanic ash, or accompanying earthquakes. The attractions of this theory are lessened by the dating for the Thera catastrophe; Marinatos' excavations at Akrotiri on Thera have revealed no material later than LM IA (c. 1500 B.C.), some 50 years too early to account for the fall of Crete. Akrotiri, it is true, seems to have been abandoned before the volcano blew up, since there have been no human remains found in the town, but there is no clear indication of the length of time the town lay empty before the final disaster. It seems safe to say, however, that Thera must have played at least an indirect role in the fall of Crete. It is possible that earthquakes resulting from the explosion could have caused considerable damage on Crete; a tidal wave may well have destroyed the Minoan fleet with which the Cretans maintained their active trade in the Mediterranean. The ash fall may have disrupted agriculture for a number of years after the eruption, as well. If the economy, which seems to have been based on a combination of trade and agriculture, was adversely affected, political unrest may have followed. The Mycenaeans at least took advantage of the situation to gain control of Crete and her Mediterranean trade routes. There is no satisfactory answer to this problem, but perhaps no single factor should be sought for the collapse of so complex a civilization as the Minoan.

Whatever caused the destruction of the other Cretan sites, the fall of Knossos remains in dispute. Evans assigned this destruction to the end of the LM II period (c. 1400), although he found much evidence for reoccupation by "squatters" in LM III. This view remained unopposed until a British philologist, L.R. Palmer, studying the Linear B tablets, reexamined the evidence for their dating and concluded that Evans had misinterpreted and even misrepresented his findings. Having checked the findspots for the tablets in the notebooks and daybooks kept by Evans and Mackenzie, Palmer concluded that they were found in association with pottery and sealings of LM IIIB (c. 1200 B.C.), a date more in keeping with their linguistic similarities to the Pylos tablets of about 1230 B.C. A number of British archaeologists who have excavated extensively at Knossos, including Hood, Boardman, and Popham, have also reexamined the excavation records and the material from the dig now in the Stratigraphic Museum at Knossos, and their findings seem to vindicate Evans. Through this heated debate much new information has come to light about the nature of Evans' excavation, which was not carried out and recorded with the precision practiced by archaeologists today. Considerable evidence has been lost, and there is little hope of a resolution to the controversy on the basis of the records that Evans and Mackenzie kept. Palmer's theory cannot be proven wrong, but new studies of material from the palace and new findings by M.R. Popham have suggested a mediating solution. Popham has gathered together pottery in the Stratigraphic Museum which can be shown to be from close destruction deposits from buildings around the palace (Popham 1970a); on the basis of these deposits he has concluded that these buildings, and probably the palace itself, fell early in LM IIIA:2 (c. 1375). His exploration of the "Unexplored Mansion" has provided evidence for a LM II destruction in addition to one in LM IIIA, a finding which suggests that there was some destruction in the palace itself in LM II, even if it was not the final one, as Evans believed. Although many still question the evidence and look for more proof from the palace, it seems likely that Knossos suffered damage in LM II, met its final destruction in LM IIIA: 2, and was reoccupied throughout LM IIIB.

The last period of the Minoan Bronze Age, LM III, still remains shadowy, and our understanding of it rests upon the interpretation of the situation at Knossos. Palmer would have us believe that this was a period of great prosperity at Knossos, but this picture does not fit with what is known about the rest of Crete in LM III. Elsewhere this was obviously a time of danger and discord and considerable impoverishment; remains of settlements are few, and most of the material comes from poor but plentiful larnax burials. A small-scale reoccupation at Knossos is more in keeping with this picture. It is even possible that the center of power shifted from Knossos to Chania in the West, where a LM III "palace" has been uncovered.

April 1979   Leslie Preston Day
                                              College of Wooster

A HANDBOOK
TO THE
PALACE OF MINOS
AT
KNOSSOS

Arthur J. Evans

Photograph of Sir Arthur Evans by the Northern
Entrance Passage of the Palace

A HANDBOOK
TO THE
PALACE OF MINOS
AT
KNOSSOS

WITH ITS DEPENDENCIES

By

J. D. S. PENDLEBURY

CURATOR

With a Foreword by
SIR ARTHUR EVANS

FOREWORD

IN fulfilment of my own desires, Mr. Pendlebury
has excellently carried out the plan of a summary
guide to the House of Minos and its immediate surroundings. In the works of reconstitution, which here
so necessarily followed that of the spade, the object of
affording an intelligible picture to the visitor had been
constantly kept in view. The replacement where
possible for sites of the fallen frescoes from the walls by
Monsieur Gilliéron's admirable restorations has supplied some samples at least of the original brilliant
decoration.

It is true that the existing remains of the building,
once with tiers of upper stories on all sides, leave vast
lacunas. The name 'Labyrinth' indeed, which itself
stands for the 'House of the *labrys*' or sacred double
axe of old Cretan and Anatolian cult, has led to
much popular misconception. But the idea of a
maze—to which the complex impression given by
parts of the basements might seem to lend some support—was far from the conception of its builders.
The Palace itself, and notably the *piano nobile* of the
West Quarter, was a crescendo of spacious corridors,
peristyles, and halls served beyond by a stately staircase. The 'Grand Staircase' again of the East Quarter,
where the main approach was from above, was of a
unique quality amongst ancient buildings. On the other
hand, the arrangement of the reception rooms in the
more public suites of state usage and the more private
section where we may place the quarters of the women
and children is a masterpiece of architectural planning.

It is now some forty years since—lured by the visions
of the earliest folk traditions of Greece and encouraged

by such indications as were to be extracted from seal-stones and the signs of an unknown script—I first explored the site, at a time when, though minor relics of great promise abounded, there was nothing visible above ground beyond the tumbled remains of a wall above the southern slope.

The work of the spade has now brought out the essential underlying truth of the old traditions that made Knossos—the home of Minos and Daedalos—the most ancient centre of civilized life in Greece and with it, of our whole Continent. It may be confidently said indeed, that no equal plot of Earth's surface has been productive in such various directions of so many unique records bearing on our earliest culture. Not only have we here the first evidences of an advanced linear script, but architecture is already fully developed on novel lines, and with a no less original form of fresco decoration carried to great perfection, while masterpieces in sculpture and moulding have here come to light—from the ivory figure of the ᵢₑaping youth to the forepart of the charging bull in painted stucco from the Northern Portico and the high reliefs of parts of athletic human figures from the Great East Hall—which for instantaneous spirit and truth to natural forms have in their own line never been surpassed.

The originals of these must be visited in the Museum at Candia. Though of old a Palace, the 'Labyrinth' of which in spite of clearing and partial reconstitution we have only to-day a fragment of a fragment, is discontinuous in many directions and in places artificially linked. The visitor who wishes to explore its full circuit still needs the guidance that of old was provided by Ariadne's clew.

ARTHUR EVANS

PREFACE

IT has been evident for some time that there ought to be a short guide to Knossos. Not only is the owner of a 1909 *Baedeker* liable to be entirely at sea and to wander in a state of complete bewilderment round a labyrinth in many respects unrecognizable, but the fortunate possessors of the *Palace of Minos* have hesitated before hiring the pack animal necessary for the transport of that monumental work round the site.

Of course there is only one man who could have written this guide as it ought to have been written—Sir Arthur Evans—but in view of the Herculean labours in which he is engaged, I hope that visitors will excuse my temerity in making the attempt. How great my debt has been both to Sir Arthur and to Dr. Mackenzie only I can say. Without their guidance I should have been as completely lost as Theseus without the clew of Ariadne.

The plan of the guide is as follows. I have first given an introductory Section on the history of the site, mainly from the point of view of the architectural development of the Palace. This, I think, was inevitable. Nobody wants either to be unexpectedly faced with a totally meaningless combination of letters such as 'Late M.M. III *b*' or to be held up while going round the site by having to read a lot of information, mostly quite irrelevant to his present position, about the general layout of the Palace at a particular period. I have therefore set this section first.

Then comes the grand tour of the Palace proper, by what experience has proved the best route. Lastly the outlying buildings are described.

The plan has the route adopted marked with arrows, and there are a few photographs to assist in the identification of landmarks.

I must apologize for addressing the visitor throughout in the second person. There are two other methods, first the impersonal 'one', which always seems so lonely, secondly the use of 'we', which is undoubtedly the cause of so many single visitors looking uneasily over their shoulders for some unseen companion.

The excavation of the Palace of Minos at Knossos is one of the most important historical events of the century. Schliemann, with his extraordinary *flair*, had intended to dig here, but at that time the political and other difficulties to be faced were insuperable. Sir Arthur Evans had spent some years travelling in the island, collecting seal-stones and evidences of the prehistoric script which they betrayed. In 1894 he had gained a foothold on the site, and when conditions became easier, on the arrival of Prince George, in 1900 he began the systematic excavation of the site. At first a Cretan Exploration Fund was formed, but for many years now Sir Arthur has borne the expense as well as the glory of the work.

Thanks to his labours and those of his assistant, Dr. Duncan Mackenzie, the prehistoric civilization of Crete has been revealed. His fellow workers in the field of Minoan archaeology have made discoveries of the utmost importance for the illumination of particular periods and sites; but nowhere, save at Knossos, is the whole evidence to hand, and if Knossos was the only site excavated we should still have a clear historical outline.

The difficulties of excavation have been many. Succeeding periods have left succeeding floor levels which must be disentangled, and the mere technical problems, such as the clearing of the Grand Staircase, were enormous.

With a building such as this, rising many stories in height, it has always been a question of how to preserve the evidence of upper floors. This has been solved by roofing in various parts of the palace and by raising to their proper level the door-jambs, column-bases, and paving-blocks which had fallen into the rooms below.

Without restoration the Palace would be a meaningless heap of ruins, the more so because the gypsum stone, of which most of the paving slabs as well as the column-bases and door-jambs are made, melts like sugar under the action of rain, and would eventually disappear completely. The accuracy of the restorations has been ensured by careful study of the evidence during the course of excavation. The yellow brown concrete beams follow the same 'chases' as their charred wooden originals. The shape and decoration of the columns, the architraves, and cornices have been taken from frescoes as well as from actual evidence found on the spot.

In conclusion I may give the following chronological table which embodies the results of thirty years' work and is now generally accepted. It is based mainly on the changes in pottery, which, in the absence of written records that we can decipher, is the safest criterion of date. But it must always be remembered that the periods are not separate watertight compartments; they often slide imperceptibly one into the next. It is not reported that Minos declared, *I'm tired of Middle Minoan III, let Late Minoan I begin!*

The term 'Minoan', it should be explained, is a

convenient one which is used to describe the whole of the Copper and Bronze Age in Crete. It is derived, of course, from the famous king Minos.

CHRONOLOGICAL TABLE

	NEOLITHIC		PREDYNASTIC PERIOD IN EGYPT
B.C. 3500 (c.)			
	EARLY MINOAN I.		Protodynastic Period in Egypt.
2800			
		II.	Roughly parallel in date with the
2400	(E.M.)		Sixth Dynasty in Egypt.
		III.	
2200			
	MIDDLE MINOAN I.		Hammurabi, c. 2100.
2000			
	(M.M.)	II.	Roughly parallel in date with the
1800			Twelfth Dynasty in Egypt.
		III.	
1580			
	LATE MINOAN I a.		
1500		I b.	Parallel with reign of Thothmes III.
1450	(L.M.)	II.	Mainly a Knossian pottery style, paralleled elsewhere by a late phase of L.M. I b ('L.M. I c.'). Palace at Knossos destroyed in latter half of Amenhotep III's reign. c. 1400.
1400			
		III.	
1100			

The positive dating is obtained by parallel finds of Egyptian objects in Crete and of Minoan objects in Egypt, for the later chronology of Egypt is now practically fixed.

Lastly as to further reading. I have already mentioned the monumental publication of the site, which is still in progress—*The Palace of Minos* by Sir Arthur Evans. Less specialized—more general—are the late

Dr. Hall's books, *Aegean Archaeology*, *The Civilisation of Greece in the Bronze Age*. Best of all short works is *Crete the Forerunner of Greece*, by E. M. and H. B. Hawes, even though it was written in 1909.

VILLA ARIADNE, KNOSSOS

1932

CONTENTS

ILLUSTRATIONS AND PLANS

AN ARCHITECTURAL HISTORY
OF THE PALACE

THE Palace at Knossos is not an artistic unity. As a Greek temple reveals the spirit of a people caught at a particular moment, so the Palace, like a Gothic cathedral or the temples of Karnak and Luxor, reveals the history and progress of its builders. Older structures are adapted to a new plan; old foundations once built over, lie in what at first seems a confusing Labyrinth where the spade has uncovered them. It must always be borne in mind, as a main cause of this multiple stratification, that Knossos lies in what, as far as human records go back, has always been a great seismic centre. Earthquake after earthquake laid the Palace low; always it rose again from its ruins more magnificent until that final disaster from which there was no recovery.

NEOLITHIC

In the Late Stone Age the low hill of Knossos was covered by a considerable settlement, traces of which are found lying to a great depth even beyond the present limits of the Palace.

Magnificently placed as Knossos is to-day, it was at that time, before centuries of occupation had raised the level of the ground, merely a very low knoll lying in a trough in the hills some three miles from the sea. Ideal as the site was in later days when it looked towards the mainland of Greece and the islands, it is hard to explain its choice by inhabitants, whose sole foreign connexion was with Egypt to the far south, on any other theory than that they were as indigenous as any race can claim to be.

However that may be, Neolithic Knossos had a long and prosperous history and was certainly the largest and most important settlement of its time in Europe and the Near East.

The houses were mainly rectangular in plan, originally perhaps of the 'but-and-ben' type, but with a considerable number of rooms opening off the main chambers. The base of the walls was rough stone-work; the upper part may have been of sundried brick. The floors were paved with pebbles or clay and red earth, and there was a fixed hearth of clay and small stones.

EARLY MINOAN I

The first part of the Early Minoan I Period at Knossos is really to be described as 'sub-neolithic'. The apparently simultaneous introduction of copper to the island from Anatolia and Egypt, and the resulting step forward in culture, took time to reach Knossos, which is hence throughout this period a little behind the east and south. One had almost said throughout the whole of the Early Minoan epoch; but this may be a misjudgement, for, as we shall see, much of the Early Minoan settlement was swept away when the first Palace was built. The few houses found below the Central Court show in their contents stronger connexions with the Nile than with Anatolia.

EARLY MINOAN II

Of the Early Minoan II Period only one house has been excavated at Knossos (to the south of the Palace). We have, however, a very good idea of the architecture of the period from the houses cleared by the late R. B. Seager at Vasilikì in the east of Crete. The houses were rectangular, possibly two or three stories high. Above a stone base the walls were constructed of sundried bricks tied together vertically and horizontally with wooden beams. The whole was covered with rough lime plaster and a fine surface wash of deep red, which formed a stucco as hard as cement. It was really a structural feature.

EARLY MINOAN III

It is in the Early Minoan III Period that we begin to find traces of monumental work. While the houses probably remained of much the same type as those of E.M. II, there appeared below what was later the South Porch of the Palace a great Hypogaeum, cut in the soft rock, some eight metres in diameter, curving up to a beehive vault about sixteen metres in height. Into it a winding stairway descended round the outside, leaving windows at intervals to look into the vault. It is possible that there may have been an exit from the floor of the Hypogaeum via a tunnel to the sloping hillside to the south, the whole forming an elaborate entrance system. Such an entrance implies something behind it worth guarding, and it therefore seems likely that there was already at this period the nucleus of the system of *Insulae* to be described below which were soon to be combined into the First Palace.

MIDDLE MINOAN I

To the very beginning of Middle Minoan I can be dated the foundation of the Palace proper at Knossos. The top of the hill was levelled into a great Central Court by sweeping away such Early Minoan structures as may have stood there and raising, by means of the debris, the north-west corner of the site, where the foundation walls of small neat stones may be seen.

c

To the north lay a long, narrow, paved court, which can now be seen projecting at either end of the Theatral Area. To the west also lay a court terraced up by the great wall which is the westernmost limit of the site. After a short time a ramp was constructed leading up to the court from the west, and, from the entrance so formed, two causeways ran across the court, one diagonally towards the north-east, the other due east to some entrance leading direct to the Central Court, past the piers of the early magazines which are still to be seen. A number of buildings, however, stood within the West Court, their basements sunk well down into the made earth inside the retaining wall. The court itself may well have stretched farther south, as far, in fact, as the heavy double wall of thick slabs which runs east and west abutting on to the present West Porch. The West Entrance of those days faced West and was approached by a causeway leading from an outer entrance in the Western Enceinte Wall along the façade of the Palace and probably lay farther back to the south. The West façade of the actual Palace itself projected beyond the present limits. Its foundations may be seen continuing the line from further north and curving in eastwards under the present façade.

The Palace itself seems to have consisted of a number of 'Insulae' which were practically independent and must have given the appearance of fortified blocks. A typical example is the 'Early Keep' to the west of the Northern Entrance. It was irregular in shape, with rounded corners, and seems to have been completely isolated. Its east wall follows the line of the later west wall of the Northern Entrance. Within this 'Keep' were six deep walled cells, called locally 'the Prisons', running down some seven or eight metres.

Another similar isolated Insula would seem to have existed to the west of the Central Court over the area now occupied by the Throne Room system. The north-east corner of this system has a rounded corner similar to those of the Keep and that in the West Court. Other Insulae were probably grouped round the Central Court. Many of the present corridors may mark the sites of older passage-ways open to the sky.

To the east the Palace seems to have sloped down in a series of narrow terraces to the great East Wall, visible at intervals below the Magazine of the Giant Pithoi and below the Hall of the Double Axes.

The latter half of Middle Minoan I showed many notable alterations. The West Façade of the Palace was pushed back at its southern end and probably generally remodelled. It is to this period that the main features of the present façade with its gypsum orthostates belongs, the early entrance direct to the Central Court being blocked. To this period, also, belongs the terrace walling of the South Front. But most important of all is the magnificent southern approach of the road which ran across the island from the south coast. This approach was remodelled in Middle Minoan III, but in its essential lines it is an M.M. I *b* construction. First the road is carried on a great viaduct, which takes two short half turns to cross the Vlychià ravine; then it divides into three, one part to run towards the Harbour Town to the north, another to the West Court, while the remainder as a great stepped portico entered the Palace at its south-west angle by some gateway now lost.

The importance of this regularization of an old trade route can hardly be over-estimated. It clearly demonstrates the traffic which ran across the island

and foreshadows the close connexions with Egypt which are a feature of the next period.

A particular characteristic of the Palace at this period was its elaborate drainage system. The pipes in particular show an advance on quite modern efforts which it is hard to believe. They are elaborately made, tapering towards one end so as to enable a greater head of water to drive through any obstruction, and neatly fitting one into the next. It is even possible that under the South Porch they may have run uphill, demonstrating that the Minoan engineers at this period had discovered the principle that water finds its own level. The incline of the section of piping that lies above the area which was occupied by the early underground vault cannot itself be regarded as evidence of this. But any conceivable access from springs in the hills around involve an ascent of the water.

MIDDLE MINOAN II

The Middle Minoan II Period is that of the consolidation of the Palace. The earlier Insulae were linked up and for the first, and indeed the only, time the Palace was a homogeneous whole.

In the West Court the early houses were razed to the level of the Court, their basements filled in, and the Court extended over the whole area, except where three deep walled pits, *Koulouras*, were sunk to receive the broken pottery from the Palace rubbish heaps.

To the north the level of the old North-West Court was considerably raised, and a broad flight of steps at the south side was constructed, on older foundations, to lead up to the causeway running to the West Porch.

Within the Palace the main feature was, as stated above, the connecting up of the earlier Insulae into a single system. The West Magazines were constructed. On the west side of the Central Court the old façade line was pushed back. The North Keep was filled in and built over; to the east of it the newly modelled North Entrance, with its full breadth, ran up to the Central Court, while a secondary entrance was planned slightly to the west, where the Lustral Area, North-West Portico, and the ramp ascending there from round the early Keep, were laid out.

To the south a porch was erected over the Early Minoan III Hypogaeum, and from it an open ramp ascended to the Central Court.

To the north-east the Royal Pottery stores and the Magazine of Giant Pithoi were built. It was in pottery the great age of polychromy.

But the crowning achievement of the period was the construction of what was later the Domestic Quarter, by means of a great cutting in the hillside immediately to the east of the Central Court, destroying the narrow terraces of the first Palace. Although this quarter was entirely remodelled in Middle Minoan III, the main lines are undoubtedly of this earlier date; for the supporting walls of the Great Cutting, the south wall of the South Light-Well of the Queen's Megaron, as well as the great walls of the Lower East-West Corridor are all datable either from the incised signs on the blocks or from the method of construction, with a clay bedding between each course. The Grand Stairway itself belongs to Middle Minoan III, but there must have been at this period something corresponding, if on a less ambitious scale.

The elaborate drainage system of this part of the Palace must also be referred to Middle Minoan II. The drains are carefully built of stone and lined with cement. At intervals gullies or minor channels run into the main system which is roughly oval in plan, its highest point being at the south end of the later Hall of Colonnades, the two channels rejoining east of the later Queen's Megaron and running out to some effluent to the east. Other drains of the same type have been discovered elsewhere in the Palace.

One of the most important pieces of evidence for the architecture of this period was discovered a little to the north of the Domestic Quarter. This is the 'Town Mosaic', a series of small faience plaques representing the façades of houses. From them we can obtain a very good idea of the domestic architecture of Middle Minoan II. They are tall and rectangular, almost towers in some cases. On the roof is usually shown an attic, sometimes with a sloping roof to let off the rain-water. In one or two cases the method above mentioned of bedding each course of stone in clay is clearly shown. The window frames are of wood and four or even six panes to a window are shown, with what appears to be some substitute for glass, perhaps oiled parchment. The absence of windows on the ground floor has been explained by the suggestion that they are houses built up against a city wall.

At the end of this period a catastrophe seems to have taken place, involving not only Knossos but also Phaestos and other sites. It appears to have been among the first of that series of earthquakes which periodically laid the Palace in ruins.

MIDDLE MINOAN III

The Middle Minoan III Period marks the beginning of a new era in the history of the Palace. It is in fact the Middle Minoan III Palace which, with small alterations, is standing to-day. Several new architectural innovations were introduced, such as the low gypsum or limestone column-base in place of the high base of variegated stone common in the preceding periods and the smooth polygonal slabs of 'almond-stone', the interstices of which were filled with red or white plaster ('mosaiko'), in place of the thick irregular limestone paving slabs ('kalderim'). Compact regular courses of masonry replace the older clay-embedded blocks. *Kasellas* or floor-cists are common. These new features taken in conjunction with a change in script and seal-types argue, if not a change of dynasty, at least a change of spirit.

The greatest changes are to be noticed on the east slope. Here the Great Cutting of Middle Minoan II was entirely remodelled on its present lines. The Grand Staircase was constructed and the whole of the Domestic Quarter is to be attributed in all essentials to this period. It may be as well here to note two of the peculiarities of Minoan architecture with which we have to deal henceforward. The first is the system of light-wells. These are particularly suited to the climate, not only admitting light to inner rooms which, in a building like the Palace, constructed on a slope, would otherwise depend on artificial illumination, but also shutting out both the piercing winds of winter and the intolerable heat of the sun in summer. The second is the downward taper of the columns characteristic of Minoan architecture. This, when one comes to think of it, is perfectly reasonable. These columns are of wood, directly descended from raw trunks which, unless planted upside-down, would be liable to sprout. Again, being of wood, the continual drip of rain after a shower would rot their bases if they were wide enough at the bottom to catch the fall. Being narrow, however, they are well out of the way. Lastly—though unless the column is very high this is not much of an argument—the part which has to carry the architrave is suitably broad, while the space between the columns, at a height where one walks between them, is appropriately larger.

Besides the plain shaft, traces have been found both of concave and convex fluting, as well as fantastic spiral grooving.

The woodwork throughout the Palace appears to have been of cypress, a proof that Pliny's phrase regarding Crete as 'the very home of cypress' is by no means an exaggeration.

The walls, as has been said above, were of fine squared masonry, often backed by rubble and with the lower courses faced with a gypsum dado.

To turn again to the plan. The lower East-West Corridor ran farther east, beyond where it was later blocked, and led to some postern at the south-east angle, towards the East Bastion, in its present state Late Minoan I. To this period belongs the open stone conduit which discharged its water into the 'Court of the Stone Spout'. The area west of this North-South Corridor gives clear indications of a great hall above. North of this lay the North-East Hall and Magazines and the North-East Entrance with its guard-room.

The Great North Entrance was narrowed at this period by the construction of bastions on either side, thus making the entrance passage the same width the whole way up. Outside the entrance the North Pillar Hall and the Propylon, through which the road from the west approached, were built.

To the west the Long Gallery of magazines was blocked by a cross wall just north of the tenth magazine, and to the south by a wall at the third magazine. The 'Enclave' thus formed is remarkable for the number of *Kasellas* or stone-lined cists which lie below the floor of the Long Corridor, and of the magazines thus enclosed which have the character of a treasury. Of a similar type are the 'Temple Repositories' containing the religious paraphernalia of some shrine.

To the north the eastern flight of steps and the 'Royal Box' were added to the Theatral Area. To the south the early broad Propylaeum was built with a typical *Kasella*, over which the wall of the present structure runs. The whole was paved in 'almond stone', and there was a dado of finely polished slabs of mottled blue-grey stone.

Just before the close of the Third Middle Minoan Period occurred a terrible earthquake which necessitated the rebuilding and restoring of most of the Palace.

In the West Court the paving was carried right over the walled *Koulouras*. The present West Porch was built and the whole West Façade was restored. The Corridor of the Procession was widened and the South Propylaeum remodelled on its present lines. The Palace on the Central Court was pushed forward and the whole Court paved in limestone. To this period belongs the general appearance of this part of the Palace with the exception of the Throne Room. The large *Kasellas* of the preceding part of Middle Minoan III were filled or paved over, and the same is true of most of the Lustral Areas.

On the whole, however, the construction of this period follows faithfully the old lines.

One point remains to be noticed. At this time begins

D

the encroachment on the Palace site of private houses. The south-west wing of the Palace (west of the Corridor of the Procession) is virtually abandoned to some powerful noble. The South House actually lies over part of the Great Stepped Portico. Most of the large private houses hitherto excavated were built at this period, including the little Palace. Methods of building construction were substantially the same as before, but some shortage of wood is evident from the habit which now begins of making the jambs of doors from tall slabs of gypsum running the whole height of the door.

LATE MINOAN I

The Late Minoan I Period has left few traces in architecture. The East Bastions of the North Entrance were partly pulled down, and the road was allowed to run over them. Towards the end of the first half of the period there seems to have been another earthquake, and a notable feature of the repairs was the plastering of whole walls, to provide a larger surface for painted decoration, of which much survives all over the Palace.

LATE MINOAN II

Late Minoan II had little to add to the Palace, except the Throne Room system which forms a small entity of its own, and a good deal of fresco work. At the end of this period, which was peculiar to Knossos, the Palace was finally destroyed, perhaps both by earthquake and the sudden onslaught of enemies somewhere at the beginning of the fourteenth century B.C. The destruction must have been irreparable, for the spirit which had treated a continuous series of disasters as inspiration for fresh splendours was crushed, and the succeeding period only shows a partial reoccupation of the site. There is, however, no real break in the course of Minoan culture, and the Residency itself may have been transferred to some other neighbouring site.

LATE MINOAN III

To this last sad period belong the Shrine of the Double Axes in the Palace proper and the 'Fetish Shrine' in the Little Palace, where the columns of the Lustral Area were walled up so that their clear impressions have survived.

For centuries the Palace lay deserted except for the ghosts of its departed glory mournfully wandering down the empty mouldering stairways, the silence broken only by the crash of falling column or block. The early Greeks considered it haunted, uncanny ground. Though all round the area Greek remains lie thick, yet within the Palace, save for the foundations of an archaic temple, no trace is found. And with that wild spring day at the beginning of the fourteenth century B.C. something went out of the world which the world will never see again; something grotesque perhaps, something fantastic and cruel, but something also very lovely.

NOTE

THE average time taken in going round the Palace by the route given is about 1¼–2 hours. The outlying houses, &c., *including the walk there and back*, take up as follows:

*1. The Little Palace { (passing the House of the Frescoes, from the Theatral Area) about 20 minutes.

*2. Royal Villa { (from the East Bastion) about 10–15 minutes.

3. House of the Sacrificed Oxen, House of the Fallen Blocks, *House of the Chancel Screen, and *South-East House } (from the south-east stairway) about 10–15 minutes.

4. *South House, *Stepped Portico, *Viaduct, *Caravanserai, and *Spring Chamber } (from south-west corner) about 30 minutes.

4a. High Priests' House and *Temple Tomb } (from Caravanserai) about 30 minutes.

5. Royal Tomb at Isopata { (from the Royal Villa) about three-quarters of an hour there, (or better separately from Candia) about half an hour there.

Those marked with an asterisk are all very well worth seeing.

The whole site *excluding* the Royal Tomb at Isopata, which is better visited either as a separate excursion from Candia or on one's way back there from Knossos, takes 2½–3½ hours, though, of course, much more might be spent on it.

For visitors with only an hour or two at their disposal one would suggest seeing as much of the Palace as possible, omitting the upper floors on the east side and, if possible, making the excursion 4–4 a above mentioned.

THE PALACE

THE Palace itself is now approached by the path which runs from the main road past the guard's house and over a modern bridge into the West Court.

This court was terraced up by means of a heavy wall, while to the right of the bridge you can see the approach that led up to it. When the court was first constructed (M.M. I, *c*. 2200 B.C.), the two causeways running across it from this entrance were laid down. One runs due east and originally entered the Palace by a doorway now blocked. The other ran diagonally across the Court to meet the causeway which skirts the West Façade of the Palace itself.

In these early days a number of houses clustered inside the wall; when the court was extended (M.M. II, *c*. 2000 B.C.) they were razed to their foundations and forgotten. Two years ago during the excavation of the two westernmost Walled Pits (*Koulouras*) traces of two of them were discovered, and the fine red-plastered floors and walls may still be seen at the bottom of the central pit (Pl. I).

These walled pits were constructed to receive the broken pottery and rubbish from the Palace heaps, and many of the finest fragments of M.M. II egg-shell ware were found in them.

In a room in one of the Late Minoan houses just to the north was a deposit of a whole series of vases connected with the worship and actual tending of the household snake, a discovery of great moment in its bearing on the primitive beginnings of the cult of the Minoan snake goddess. The 'snake tubes' here supplied for the shelter of the water-loving reptiles were themselves modelled on sections of the capacious clay waterpipes of the Palace.

Turning to the façade of the Palace it is interesting to see the way in which it reached its present form. The great foundation slabs of the façade of the first Palace (M.M. I) can be made out curving away at the south end under the present line. When, slightly later in the same period, the façade was pushed back to its present position, there was evidently some feeling that what had once formed part of the sacred Palace should not be profaned: an altar was therefore built in the deserted space to preserve its sanctity.

The present façade bears signs of the final destruction of the Palace. On one of the upright gypsum slabs you can see the mark where the end of a blazing beam rested, while all to the north is blackened by the wind-driven smoke. Now violent south winds are commonest in late April to early May, and the Athenian tradition maintained that this was the time of the year when Theseus sailed for Knossos.

Turning south you enter the Palace proper by the West Porch, with its single column and its guard-room and reception room where was probably a royal seat. The decoration of the walls during the last period of the Palace consisted of scenes taken from the bull-ring. South from here leads the Corridor of the Procession, the state entrance. It is so called from the frescoes, on its walls, of a procession of youths and maidens bringing offerings to the goddess. This corridor, which now ends abruptly, originally carried on for some fifteen paces, then turned left (clearing the present restored south-west corner) and ran along the south end of the Palace until it turned again and entered the central court near where the Priest-King fresco stands (see below, page 41). At the point, however, where it breaks off you can get a very good view across the Vlychià ravine to the Caravanserai (page 57), the Spring Chamber (page 58), and the abutment of the great paved road which ran right across the island from the south coast, along which came the merchandise from Egypt, and Pharaoh's ambassadors to Minos (Pl. X). The road ran below the Caravanserai and was carried along the huge viaduct whose massive piers can be seen, with steps between them to let through the water from the springs above. It then turned northwards and was carried across the ravine on a bridge. Here it split into three, one part skirted the Palace and ran north to the Harbour Town of Knossos, just east of modern Candia; one part seems to have entered the West Court in some way not quite clear; while the main division ascended in a great stepped portico whose foundations are still visible, to a gateway, now lost, in the south-west corner of the Palace, whence access was gained to the Corridor of the Procession. Nearer to the Palace, to the left of the approach, can be seen the South House (page 55) which encroaches on it.

Being unable to follow the corridor, you now go through the door to your left behind the red column, and take up your stand at the point where the guest would leave the Corridor of the Procession to enter the South Propylaeum (Pl. II). The south-east quarter of this has been restored; the remaining three column-bases can be seen. Originally it was wider, projecting farther east; for the sunk chest by the eastern anta runs under the present wall. The decoration of the walls consisted of a procession of young men carrying vases. The most complete of these—the famous

Cup-bearer—is in the Museum, and the replicas set up
here in their original position have been completed
from this figure and from fragments. These figures
show the ideal of Minoan youth, with their 'wasp-waists'
—still to be seen in Crete—their long black curling
locks, their kilts and metal girdles, the seal-stones on their
wrists. They bear a striking resemblance to the 'Great
Ones of Keftiu' whom we see in the Egyptian tombs
bringing presents of Minoan works of art to Pharaoh.

The great pair of horns, standing near the Propylaeum, originally crowned the south front of the
Palace.

Continuing through the Propylaeum you ascend the
open staircase, which once was flanked by colonnades,
to the 'Piano Nobile', the main floor where the state
apartments and the reception halls lay. It may seem
somewhat ambitious to have reconstructed so much
when naturally nothing was found *in situ*, but the
presence of column-bases and door-jambs, of actual
steps as well as of paving-slabs which must have fallen
from an upper story, together with the thickening of
certain walls below so as to bear the extra weight, fully
justify the attempt to make this most important part
of the Palace intelligible. In addition to this the disin-
tegration of much of the lower story made some sort
of roofing imperative.

At the top of the steps is a porch, and a vestibule,
then comes a room with three columns, to the right
of which lay a temple treasury, the marble rhytons, and
other contents of which were found below. The upper
long corridor which runs down the centre of the Piano
Nobile was open to the sky. Not only did it have to
give light to many of the rooms on either side but also
fragments of hard waterproof paving were found.

Beyond and to the left lie the Great Hall with evidence of two columns and a narrower hall with six.

You now descend the wooden stairs provided at the south end into the Long Corridor of the magazines below (Pl.II). This part of the Palace must have been usually in pitch darkness; it can only have been illuminated by lamps or torches. Below the paving of the corridor lie a number of sunken chests (*Kasellas*) and the same is the case in the magazines. These had been originally lined with lead, and there is evidence that they had been used for valuable possessions. Remains of inlaid caskets and gold foil were found in some of them. Most of the great jars, in which were the wine and the oil which formed the revenue and the exports of the merchant-princes of Knossos, have been mended and set up in their original positions. When the Palace was destroyed some of the oil caught fire and the jars overturned. The blazing oil soaked into the gypsum slabs, many of which are still black and greasy.

There are eighteen of these magazines, not counting three at the south end which were disused. The truncated pyramidal blocks of gypsum at intervals are stands for the sacred double axes, which have probably fallen from the floor above. From upper offices must have come the quantities of clay tablets inscribed in the latest linear script to the Palace (Class B) that were found here, by many regarded as the most important find of the excavation. Over fourteen hundred of these were found, belonging to numerous deposits and clearly consisting in most cases of inventories of possessions and lists of men and women. These also contained graffito sketches of many of the objects referred to, such as various forms of vases, cereals, arms, chariots, and horses. Some of them were found contained in a clay chest, and from a tradition preserved by the 'Chronicles of Dictys Cretensis' it looks as if the first discovery of Minoan tablets had been due to a great earthquake of Nero's time, resulting in the breaking open of 'a chest of tin' at Knossos containing 'lime-bark' documents in an unknown writing. The Cists of the Minoan Palace were, as we have seen, lead-lined.

At the north end of the corridor you turn right, pass the small magazine where a large deposit of hieroglyphic tablets were found, turn right again, then left until you come to a wooden door in the blank wall on your right; you turn left again opposite this door and descend by a winding ramp. To the right of this are the foundations of one of the earliest parts of the Palace, the old Keep (M.M. I). Originally it seems to have formed a sort of isolated block-house, and down below the foundations run six deep stone-lined pits. Traces were found in some of a lining of hard plaster, which might point to water-storage. For dungeons also they would have been well adapted. When the Palace, as it now stands, was built, these pits were floored over, and from this area came the frescoes known as the 'Saffron Gatherer' and the Miniature frescoes (page 39).

Passing through a door at the bottom of the ramp you emerge into the North-West Portico. To your left lies the Lustral Area, now roofed in, where those coming into the Palace by this entrance could purify themselves by descending into Mother Earth and perhaps anointing themselves with oil, for small oil flasks were found here. It is in no sense a bath, though in the Late Minoan I Period they seem to have put cleanliness before godliness, and to have filled up most of the lustral areas and converted them into baths. It can never have been filled with water—the gypsum paving and wall-slabs would not have stood it. It is purely a ceremonial Purificatory Area.

Leaving the Palace for a moment you turn west to the 'Theatral Area' (Pl. III). The flat paved area has tiers of steps on two sides, and, in a corner, a heavy bastion, perhaps the 'Royal Box'. Here, perhaps, Minos would sit to review his troops, to receive foreign envoys or the tribute from his mainland dominions, or to watch the dances we see in the Miniature frescoes (page 39) while grouped around him stands his Court. Originally it was a flat open space, for the paving runs right under the steps and reappears behind them, while an earlier paving was of an even greater extent. (A block of one of the steps has been removed to show the various earlier levels.) Later the steps leading up southwards were added, and finally the eastern flight. The idea that this was the 'dancing ground of Ariadne' cannot be maintained. We must look for that below the West slope.

From the Theatral Area you look westwards along the ancient road, the 'oldest road in Europe'. It is well paved with stone slabs and on either side are cement wings and drains. It leads to the main road north (see above, page 19) and to the Little Palace (page 50), three minutes away on the other side of the modern road. But you must imagine it not as a lonely country lane but as a main road in a busy city. On either side lie houses, the House of the Frescoes (page 50) and the Arsenal. The Palace was not isolated: it was the centre of a great city whose population can hardly have been less than 100,000 at a moderate estimate, if the extensive harbour town of which we have evidence is

included. The road itself seems narrow, but we must
remember that the horse appears very late in Crete
and that the rich people were carried in palanquins,
the stone-paved crown of the road being more of a
causeway to prevent the feet of the bearers slipping.

You now turn back and pass along the north side
of the Palace until you enter, through the foundations
of a propylaeum, the hall with massive square piers
known as the 'Customs House'. From here ascends,
direct to the Central Court, the North Entrance
(Pl. IV). When the Palace was first built, this entrance was the full width from the high wall to the
left to the back wall of the restored portico on the right.
Perhaps some fear of a swift raiding party from the coast
caused them in Middle Minoan III to narrow it down
by means of throwing out bastions from each wall.
Above these bastions are colonnades, the walls decorated
with reliefs in which we may perhaps see the origin of
the 'Vapheio cups', with the decoy cow and the cowboys.
That to the west has been restored to cover a reproduction of the Charging Bull relief which stood here.
A staircase farther up the ramp leads on to the Portico.
This reproduction is built up of many fragments. The
leaves of the olive tree are in some cases painted in
relief and in some cases on the flat. They show three
colours, the dark green of the top of the leaf, the pale
green of the back, and the red of autumn. The bull
itself was standing when the Greeks came, for it was
found fallen at a higher level than Greek remains. It
must have lent some colour to the story of the Mino-
taur. All the Palace, in fact, seems to have been
regarded as haunted, uncanny ground, for while immediately outside its bounds Greek remains from the
Geometric period onwards lie thick, yet in the Palace

itself, apart from one small shrine (page 41), not a trace of Greek habitation is found.

It is worth noting in passing that the masons' marks on the blocks of this sea-gate of Knossos are in the form of a trident.

As you go up the ramp you see gradually rising the mass of Mount Juktas where the 'lying Cretans' vainly said Zeus was buried. From some way farther west its shape is like the fine bearded head of a reclining god.

The Central Court divides the official and the state quarters of the Palace to the west from the more private and domestic quarters to the east (Pl. VIII). When the Palace proper was founded (M.M. I), all the buildings which had once stood here were swept away and the present Court was made and levelled, the debris being used to raise the level of the north-west corner of the Palace. As a result, you now stand immediately on the Neolithic remains, which descend in some places as much as twenty feet. Traces of the paving of the court can be seen here and there. In the north-west corner, in 'a M.M. II' stratum, was found part of the statue of an Egyptian official called User, perhaps ambassador to the Court of Minos.

The first group of rooms on the west side of the Court consists of the Throne Room and the other rooms connected with it, constructed in the last days of the Palace (L.M. II).

Fronting on to the Court is an antechamber with a stone bench on the north and the south walls, and a reproduction in wood of the throne in the next room, which has been set up where charred remains suggested its position. Next comes the 'Throne Room' (so called) proper. To the right stands the gypsum throne of Minos where it was found. Flanking it are reproductions of the crouching griffins, fragments of which were found lying here and on either side of the door into the shrine beyond. Facing the throne is a sunken 'Lustral Area' for purificatory purposes—not a bath as first supposed. There is every reason for supposing that this chamber served a ritual purpose—probably as a kind of Consistory for the Priest-Kings. There are signs here of a sudden catastrophe in the middle of some ritual of anointing, flat alabastra lying on the floor beside the entrance together with an overturned oil-jar for filling them.

Beyond the Throne Room proper seems to be a small shrine with a ledge, on which fragments of cult objects and ornaments were found. To the right of that is a small exhibition of pottery, while to the left is a room from which you can look into a small chamber with stools, a plaster ledge, and what may be a plaster hearth. We know it as the 'kitchen'.

The whole of this group of rooms forms a self-contained system, and it is probable that the king retired here for ceremonies that may have lasted for some days.

From just outside the north-east corner of the ante-room a spiral staircase runs up to the second floor. The rounded corner within which it ascends is a relic of the first (M.M. II) Palace which survived down to the final destruction. On the second floor have been reconstructed a terrace and a series of rooms corresponding to those below. Immediately above the Throne Room have been hung a series of reproductions of various frescoes found in the Palace and in a house nearby. Opposite the door hangs the group known as the 'Ladies in Blue' found on the east side of the Palace. South of the door is first a charming little work from the House of the Frescoes (see page 50)

known as the 'Captain of the Blacks', the smart young
Minoan subaltern leading his black Sudani troops at
the double. Beyond that is the fantastic fresco the
'Saffron Gatherer', the earliest example of pictorial
work we have (M.M. II) (Pl. XI). It came from the
area above the deep walled pits (see page 34). On the
north wall of the room are two scenes from the Miniature Frescoes, which were found in the same area,
though they are of later date (M.M. III–L.M. I).
They show very well the impressionistic skill of the
artist in portraying crowds. The way in which a number of heads and figures of men are drawn on a general
red background, with splodges of white to show the
feminine element, is very effective. Note also the excited
arms flung up on the sky-line. The dance shown in one
of the pictures is evidently taking place in some such
spot as the Theatral Area (see page 35), for the causeways are shown and the spectators seem to be grouped
in tiers one above the other. North of the door comes
a very spirited scene from the bull-ring (see page 46)
of which the Minoans were so fond (Pl. XIII). Both
men and women indulged in this dangerous sport, and
if the game really consisted of catching the bull's horns
and somersaulting on to his back and off again, it
must have required a great deal of skill and training.
This fresco came from the east side of the Palace. Lastly
come three more pictures from the House of the
Frescoes. They are all studies of animal and plant
life: the blue monkeys in the gardens and the singing
bird.

Passing through this room and those beyond you
come out into the Upper Long Corridor again (page
32). Turn to the left and then to the left again until
you are on the landing of the broad flight of steps

leading down to the Central Court. Before actually going down you should look at one of the gypsum blocks to the left of the *ascending* flight on which are clearly seen the marks of steps, thus giving evidence for yet a further story.

On entering the Central Court again you turn to the right, and on the foundations of the frontage you can make out the lower parts of the façade of a shrine. Originally there were two columns on either side of a central block, which in its turn supported a fifth. This arrangement is shown in one of the frescoes. Only the slightest traces, however, now remain.

Beyond the shrine you descend a few steps into an open court—the Lobby of the Stone Seat. To the right of this is first the Room of the Tall Pithos and beyond that the Temple Repositories. Here were stored the treasures and offerings of the shrine. In one of the two big cists was found the famous faience figurine of the Snake Goddess with her attendant, now in the Museum. These big cists were covered over later and three smaller ones substituted, of which the central one is still in position.

West of the open Court are two rooms with square piers in the middle (Pl. IV). These two Pillar Crypts seem to have had a sacred character, for not only is the double-axe sign scratched many times on each pillar, but round the bases are channels and containers for the blood of sacrifices or other liquid offerings (cf. Royal Villa, page 53; Temple Tomb, page 60). North of the first of these crypts is a room known as the Vat Room.

You now go back to the Lobby of the Stone Seat and leave it again by the double-doors to the south. A passage to the right shows the piers of the magazines

of the first Palace with the ✚ sign scratched on them
as a mason's mark.

After ascending the shallow flight of steps straight
ahead, you come to an open space which was later
occupied by the Greek Temple—the only later building
found on the Palace site proper (cf. page 37).

You now return to the Central Court to the south
of the verandah, which probably ran the whole way
round.

Before crossing to the Eastern or Domestic Quarters
you should look at the reconstructed entrance of the
Procession Corridor (see page 30) into the Central
Court. Near this point the Priest-King fresco was found
and a replica has been fixed in its original position
(Pl. V). This painted relief shows the Minoan ideal of
a prince, with the waving peacock feathers of his crown
and his collar of fleur-de-lis; who knows it is not some
order of Minoan chivalry? Like an Egyptian Pharaoh
he is shown wearing a much simpler form of dress
than his subjects, a mere loin-cloth, in fact, clasped
about him by a thick girdle. He seems to be leading
something or some one, perhaps, as we see on gems, a
griffin. And about him are the fantastic flowers and
butterflies of a Minoan Paradise.

You now cross the Central Court to the top of the
Grand Staircase. The stone tower on the way is not
ancient. It was originally three stories high so as to
command a view of the whole site before so much
roofing in had been done. It is now the architect's
office.

The presence of step marks on the gypsum landing
block show again that yet higher stories existed to the
east.

The Grand Staircase itself is one of the greatest

marvels of antiquity (Pl. III). Five flights have been preserved *in situ*, and, with its broad shallow treads, it must have been a fit passage for processions and pageants.

On the east wall of the balcony of the first landing has been placed a replica of the Shield Fresco, showing the great figure-of-eight war shields hanging over a spiral frieze. The original fragments were found in a space below. The markings on the shields represent the dappling of the bull's hide from which they were made; the yellow band down the middle is the bristly hair which runs down the centre of the back, as is shown in the Toreador Fresco (cf. page 39 above). The stitches for a double thickness of hide where the shield was most likely to be pierced are also shown. This balcony is known as the Upper Hall of the Colonnades.

Descending to the bottom of the Grand Staircase, you enter the Hall of Colonnades proper. The open light-well here is a typical feature of Minoan architecture. It successfully lights and airs any number of stories, while it keeps out the biting winds and the scorching sun, obviating the necessity of outside windows.

Leaving the Hall of Colonnades by a door in the north-east corner you go a few paces along the lower East-West Corridor and turn to the right into the Hall of the Double Axes. This has received its name from the frequent occurrence of that symbol as a mason's mark on the blocks of the wall to your right as you enter.

To your left is the outer Hall of the Double Axes, a large rectangular room the partitions of which could be separately closed (Pl. VI). There are holes for the hinges of doors, and it is extremely probable that oiled parchment was used to glaze the casements above the doors. In this room was found a spiral frieze identical with that from the Upper Hall of the Colonnades, but without the shields. It is a reasonable assumption that in this case the shields themselves were hung on the walls, and replicas have been placed here. These, of course, would be of oxhide, and their curious shape is due to the necessity for having a glancing surface at every point, since the number of thicknesses necessary to offer resistance to a direct blow would render the shields impossibly heavy.

A wooden throne has been placed here corresponding to the traces of a plaster-backed throne in the next room (beneath the glass case).

There are two light-wells, and from the southernmost a good view is obtained up the ravine of the Kairatos River to the Venetian aqueduct.

Returning to the inner hall, you leave it by a door in the south wall which leads, via a dog's-leg corridor, into the Queen's Megaron (Pl. VI). This winding passage, which must have given a certain amount of privacy, is lined with tall slabs of gypsum.

The Queen's Megaron, also, has two light-wells, and, on a small scale, corresponds to the Hall of the Double Axes. Over the entrance door is hung a reproduction of the Dolphin Fresco, with its dolphins and fishes and sea-urchins. A frieze of dancing-girls seems later to have formed part of the decoration. One of the figures has been copied and hangs here.

The small room to the west is the bathroom. The bath has been considerably restored in plaster, and the curious convex fluting of the column has been taken from impressions discovered in the Little Palace (see page 51). A paving block has been removed to show the earlier phases, for the whole of this wing of the Palace was continually being altered or restored (see above, page 23).

From the south-west corner of the Queen's Megaron you pass through the Corridor of the Painted Pithos into the Queen's toilet room. This room is lit by a small light-well, known from the masons' marks found there as the Court of the Distaffs. In one corner is a plaster base, while holes in the wall above, which connect with cisterns on a higher level, suggest that there may have been some system of running water. Against the east wall is the closet with arrangements for flushing, a connected system of drains and sewers and traces of a wooden seat. The elaborate drainage system of this part of the Palace is very well seen in the recess at the beginning of the dark corridor that you next pass through. The general plan was roughly oval in shape, the two arms meeting east of the Queen's Megaron and running out to some effluent on the east slope. At intervals there are minor sewers and man-holes for inspection.

The room to the right of the dark passage, labelled the 'Lair', and now given over to the storage of pottery fragments, was probably a Treasury, while under the narrow stairway to the left were found the famous Ivory Leapers of the Candia Museum as well as other fragments which show the skill of the Minoan artist in such delicate work. Connected with the Treasury was the largest of the inscribed clay tablets found in the Palace giving in three sections consisting, together, of eighteen lines long lists of persons whose names are marked by the ideographs of 'Man' and 'Woman'.

The passage leads you again to the Hall of Colonnades and again you make as if you were going to the

Hall of the Double Axes. Instead of turning to the right, however, carry straight on and turn to the left into a small lobby, whence you reach the Eastern Portico of the Palace. Looking back from here you can see a large block of gypsum above a square pier. This block was projecting out of the ground before excavation began, and has been preserved in its original position. Behind this Eastern Portico are two rooms, one known as the Room of the Stone Pier, one containing lumps of Spartan basalt (*Lapis Lacedae-monius*) which had been imported and was actually being worked when disaster overtook the Palace.

You have now left the domestic part of the Palace. All to the north was devoted to the craftsmen, the potters, and lapidaries. Looking down to the east you can see the massive East Wall, a relic of the first Palace which sloped down in narrow terraces.

The next room, reached by rather a scramble, was known as the 'School Room'. It has benches on three sides and plastered receptacles by them. More probably, however, it was some potter's or craftsman's workroom, formed by building partition walls across a large hall. North of this is the open Court of the Stone Spout, so called from the spout which drained off the rain-water from the roof of the Great East Hall above and led it to the blind well in this Court. On the wall above is a fine example of a column-base in breccia. The tallness of it betrays its early date (M.M. II).

Immediately to the north are the 'Giant Pithoi' (Pl. VII). These vast jars, big enough to hide all the Forty Thieves at once, are again relics of the earlier (M.M. II) Palace. Though they could never have been transported once they were *in situ*, they proudly display a multitude of handles and knobs to facilitate handling, as well as a decoration of rope-pattern.

You turn now and descend to the East Bastion, where there is a strongly protected postern gate. The interest of this entrance lies in the elaborate method of automatically checking the flow of rain-water in the open conduit which runs down beside the steps. Instead of allowing the water to come down a plain incline, gathering speed the whole way and splashing over when it comes to a corner, the engineers led the water down in a series of small waterfalls; at the bottom of each it was checked, with the result that it reached the corner at only half-speed and turned it without spilling a drop. Near the bottom are two square basins where sediment was allowed to deposit before the clean water flowed out below. Sir Arthur attractively suggests that the Palace laundry may have been here. (From here to the Royal Villa, see below page 52, three minutes.)

On the flat stretch of land between here and the river—the only suitable space in the district—Sir Arthur believes the Bull-Ring to have been, the ring where the foreign tribute of youths and maidens, sent from the mainland dominions of Minos, showed their skill with the Bull of Minos.

From the East Bastion you ascend again past the Giant Pithoi till you come out on to a flat paved corridor where a grating shows the drain-pipes of the first Palace, with their carefully tapering shape to ensure a greater head of water driving through any stoppage. This Corridor of the Draughtboard was where the inlaid gaming table, now in the Museum, was found. On one side lies the North-East Hall, on the other, at a lower level, a series of openings with grooves for sliding partitions, which may be kennels, and beyond them the Royal Pottery stores where the thin egg-shell ware of Middle Minoan II style was discovered.

From the Corridor of the Draughtboard you turn south. There are three openings. The left-hand, eastern one, is an open court in which lies the upper channel of the rain-water conduit which comes out in the Court of the Stone Spout (see page 45). The central door leads to the Magazine of the Medallion Pithoi of which several have been restored. They are mainly important for the light they shed on a particularly debatable point in the history of Mycenae.

The western door leads into the Corridor of the Bays, the massive piers of which probably supported some heavy weight in the hall above, whose general outline can be made out on the plan by following the heaviest of the basement walls. In this Great East Hall, there is reason to believe, a colossal female statue, probably the great Minoan Goddess, once stood, whose bronze locks were discovered below, as well as masses of charred wood. To this Hall must have belonged the series of high reliefs in plaster taken from agonistic scenes and representing the highest development of Minoan glyptic art.

Passing through the Corridor of the Bays, you arrive again in the Upper Hall of the Colonnades. Leave the Shield Fresco on your right and, after going a few steps along the Middle East-West Corridor, turn right, into the Upper Hall of the Double Axes. Here the door-jambs which were found fallen below have been put back into their original position and a small piece of Late Minoan II fresco, showing part of a bull's leg, has been protected.

The door in the south-west corner leads into the Upper Queen's Megaron, passing the Queen's private flight of stairs. The arrangement of the rooms appears to be identical, save that above the Room of the Plaster Couch is a room with a stone seat on the west wall and traces of a w.c. in the south-west corner.

Another slight scramble leads you south to a small passage off which open two rooms which have been roofed over. In this passage were found the Lily Jars, small jars of pinkish clay with lilies in white (M.M. III).

The first of the rooms opening off this passage is the bathroom, in which is preserved a very graceful bath decorated with sprays of grass in the style typical of Late Minoan I *a*. On the rim are what looks suspiciously like supports for a sponge-rail! The door seems to have had a low gypsum barrier and the room has been flippantly called the 'Nursery'. The second room contains three jars. One has a pierced spout, another has a spout, but it is not pierced right through, the third merely has the lip pulled out into a sort of knob. What an archaeological problem! How long did they take to forget how to make a spout? or, alternatively, how long did they take to learn how to make a spout? As a matter of fact all three jars are contemporaneous! The smallest has a pierced spout because it was small enough to be tilted to pour out its contents. The other two were too big to be tilted and were therefore carelessly finished off.

Round behind these two rooms, opening off the passage known as the Corridor of the Sword Tablets, from clay inventories found here, is a small shrine of the Double Axes, which has been roofed in (Pl. VII). It is a sad little building, constructed by men of Late Minoan III, after the destruction of the Palace. On the edge are the plaster horns and rude statuette of votaries, while in front are the tripod and the offerings. There is every sign here of a sudden catastrophic interruption of the ritual.

South of this is another Lustral Area and the remains of a staircase and a light area.

Looking over the wall of this light area, you can see, in one of the houses below, the huge blocks shaken by the earthquake of Middle Minoan III from the Palace façade. (For the House of the Fallen Blocks, the House of the Chancel Screen, the South-East House, the House of the Sacrificed Oxen, and the Monolithic Pillar Basement, see page 53 et sqq.)

Lastly, before leaving the Palace itself you walk along the South Corridor, into which led the South Porch, near which fragments of the old road can still be seen. Underneath this South Porch, in Early Minoan times, was a large subterranean vault, cut in the rock, some forty feet high with a staircase running round outside it. It was evidently a secret or, at any rate, a heavily guarded entrance.

From here you pass along the South Front until you come to the south-west corner, whence you can either ascend back into the West Court or—I hope—go on south to the South House, the Caravanserai, and the Temple Tomb (see page 55).

THE DEPENDENCIES OF THE PALACE

1. THE LITTLE PALACE (PASSING THE HOUSE
OF THE FRESCOES)

*T*HE *House of the Frescoes* lies some eighty yards from the Theatral Area to the left of the ancient road. It is in the south-east corner of the cutting, and dates from the transition period M.M. III *b*–L.M. I *a*, i.e. *c*. 1600 B.C. The other houses are earlier (M.M. III *a*, i.e. *c*. 1750 B.C.). The entrance is in a small wing which projects north and contained, in addition to the entrance lobby, a doorkeeper's room to the left. From the lobby are entered two passage rooms to the east, and to the west a long narrow room which, in its turn, gave on to the main room of the house in which was found the stack of frescoes. These thin fragile slabs of painted plaster had been carefully piled here in layers, and when, with infinite labour, they had been separated, strengthened, and fitted together they gave an idea of the brilliance of the decoration of even a small house. Reproductions of some of them are in the room above the Throne Room (see page 38). The originals are in the Museum. South of the Room of the Frescoes lie three more rooms, in the easternmost of which occurred a number of vase fragments decorated with designs of double axes.

Leaving the House of the Frescoes, you continue along the ancient road, passing on your right the depression which marks the site of the 'Arsenal' which has now been filled in, until you climb up to the modern road. On the far side of the road, just north of the village street, a flight of steps leads up the far bank and thence over a small bridge into the Little Palace.

The Little Palace is the second largest building hitherto excavated at Knossos (Pl. VIII). It is roughly ninety yards by thirty. Much of the east side has unfortunately disappeared, including the actual entrance, but enough remains to show us a most stately suite of reccption rooms which the Palace itself cannot rival.

From the entrance hall four shallow flights of stairs lead up into the 'Hall of the Peristyle' beyond which was the Great Megaron. These rooms were bordered to the east by a corridor whose outer border consisted of two groups of columns between square piers. Whether there were further buildings to the east, or whether they stood on the edge of a terrace, it is impossible to say.

Off the north-west corner of the Great Megaron opens a paved lavatory with a stone sink. West of the Hall of the Peristyle is the stairway, two flights of which still remain. West again is a doorway whose jambs, instead of being constructed of wood resting on gypsum bases, are of gypsum the whole height, a symptom perhaps of the gradual deforestation of the island which seems to have begun about the period the Little Palace was being built (M.M. III *b*–L.M. I *a*).

North of this, part of the building has been roofed over, and is entered from the west. There is a step on which to stand in order to look into the Lustral Area. On the destruction of Knossos generally, at the end of Late Minoan II, the Little Palace was reoccupied by 'squatters'. They divided up the larger rooms by building partition walls, and in this case they walled up the space between the columns of the East Balustrade. The wooden columns have perished, but their impressions remain and can be seen. It is from these column impressions with their convex fluting that the column in the bathroom of the Queen's

Megaron was taken. At the same time, the Lustral Area did not lose its sanctity, for it was used as a shrine, and on the stone balustrade were placed the 'fetish' figures of natural stone, the objects of adoration of the period of reoccupation.

Across the whole southern end of the building run a series of Pillar Crypts. The two most easterly lie at a lower level; between the pillars are the stone-vats. The south-westerly crypt adjoined a small stone shaft in which was found the magnificent steatite rhyton in the shape of a bull's head, as well as a number of other ritual vessels.

Separated by a narrow lane from the west wall of the Little Palace is the façade of a yet larger building, the 'Unexplored Mansion'.

2. THE ROYAL VILLA

The Royal Villa is most easily approached from the East Bastion (page 46). You follow the path to the left until it forks, then you take the lower one and arrive in three minutes from the Palace.

The Villa is set back into a cutting in the hillside overlooking the Kairatos ravine. You first enter a Light-Well, to the left of which lies the Megaron. Fronting on to the Light-Well are two columns, and the Megaron, entered from here, is divided by a row of three doors into two sections. At the west end, backing up against the retaining wall, is the throne, set back in a sort of apse behind a balustrade supporting two columns. In front of the throne is a lamp of purple gypsum. Above the throne was probably some sort of light-well, roofed over at a higher level, so that there could be verbal communication between the seat of honour and the rooms above.

North of the Megaron is a Pillar Crypt with a single square pier, round which are channels and cists to catch blood or other liquid offerings (cf. page 40). From this crypt a flight of stairs communicates with the upper story. In the top course of the masonry of this crypt can be seen the slots for the great cypress beams which supported the ceiling.

South of the Megaron is a passage from which ascends a flight of stairs. As a matter of fact, the excavation of the Villa was begun by tunnelling along this passage and up the stairs. Ten stairs up is a landing, just above which was found a magnificent jar with painted decorations in relief, consisting of clumps of papyrus, belonging to the Late Minoan II Period. Above the landing the stairway divides into two separate wings to reach the upper story. This upper story seems to have followed the lines of the lower one for the most part, and it has been so restored. It is probable that the main entrance to the building was on this level, for a branch of the causeway which runs above the Theatral Area would, if prolonged, strike the middle of the west wall of the Villa. In any case, Sir Arthur is justified in seeing in it a dependency of the Great Palace.

3. THE HOUSE OF THE SACRIFICED OXEN, HOUSE OF THE FALLEN BLOCKS, HOUSE OF THE CHANCEL SCREEN, SOUTH-EAST HOUSE

The first two of these houses are M.M. III constructions, overthrown by the great earthquake about the middle of M.M. III *b*. As a result, only the basement rooms remain. They lie just below the south-east angle of the Palace. In the first of these was found the remains of a sacrifice, a tripod altar, and the horns of

a Urus bull. Into the second house had been hurled
a number of huge blocks from the Palace façade.

The House of the Chancel Screen which adjoins these
has been partially covered over. It, too, seems to have
been deserted after the earthquake. Its entrance has
disappeared, but probably a passage led to the steps
which ascend into the Central Hall, off which the
Megaron opens to the north. At the west end of the
Megaron is a dais for a seat of honour, railed off by
a balustrade on which stood two columns (cf. Royal
Villa, page 52). This has given the house its name,
and even the workmen called it the 'House of the
Priest' (τοῦ Παπᾶ τὸ Σπίτι).

In the middle of the west side of the house is a Pillar
Crypt with one square pier; while close to the entrance
is a small Lustral Area.

The South-East House you descend to from the House
of the Chancel Screen by what may well have been
its original entrance, two flights of stairs. At the bottom
of these is a corridor, and to the left a Pillar Crypt with
the usual sunken cist, and, by the wall, a libation-table.
Beside the pillar is a truncated pyramidal block, the
support for a Double Axe. The crypt was lighted by
a magnificent tall lamp of purple gypsum, sculptured
in the style of an Egyptian papyrus sceptre. The
Megaron lay to the south of the House behind a
peristyle, whose tall column-bases of polychrome stone
show that they are at the beginning of the third Middle
Minoan Period, if not earlier than that. The house is
especially distinguished by the beautiful lily fresco
which was found by the staircase.

North of this house lie a number of buildings con-
temporary with the first Palace (M.M. I), most notable
of which is the monolithic pillar basement lying just

below the South Light-Well of the Hall of the Double Axes. It is a question whether these buildings ever formed part of the Palace proper.

4. THE SOUTH HOUSE, STEPPED PORTICO AND VIADUCT, CARAVANSERAI, AND SPRING CHAMBER

The South House lies just below the south-west corner of the Palace. It was evidently built soon after the disastrous earthquake towards the end of the Middle Minoan III *b* Period, for, like many buildings of that date, it encroached on what had hitherto been Palace ground; in this case on the stepped portico which led up to the main entrance from the south (Pl. IX). Very likely this practice is evidence of the rise of the power of the nobles at the expense of the king. Enough has been recovered to render the plan of two stories and a basement, and the presence of a third story certain.

Though the original entrance was probably in the south-east corner, the house is now entered direct from the causeway into a columnar hall on the middle story. By the column is a stand for a Double Axe. From the north-east corner of the room a narrow staircase, lighted by a large window, leads down to the Pillar Crypt below. The pillar is not set quite square with the room. On one side is another stand for a Double Axe; on the other, three depressions in the paving mark the site of stands for other sacred objects. In the doorway of this room was found a hoard of silver vessels originally stored in wooden chests. The next room to the east opens to the north on to a lavatory and latrine, and to the south on to a hall with three columns. North of this a passage leads to the Lustral Area. The east side of the house was probably occupied by the entrance system.

Near the Lustral Area a flight of stairs leads down to the basement. The doors at this lowest level have jambs of gypsum which run the whole height and give evidence of a certain shortage of wood in this period. It is interesting to see the primitive way of locking the door which is here adopted. A bar was slid across the door into a slot in the jamb, where it was locked by bronze pins which slid in through holes in the jamb above and below.

It is noteworthy that both this cellar and the smaller ones opening off it could only be locked from within. Were they wine cellars? The main cellar has three square piers supporting the roof, and opens directly into the smaller one, in which was found a hoard of bronze tools including a long saw. It is possible that this latter room could be entered by a trap-door from above.

The Stepped Portico lies to the right of the path as you descend from the South House. It presents at the moment a most confusing appearance. Originally it carried a great stepped approach from the lowest point visible, where the bridge-head crossing the ravine ended, up to the lost South-West Porch of the Palace. At intervals the foundations are strengthened to bear the weight of the columns which supported the roof. These columns only occurred on the western side; the eastern (nearest) side rose up a blank wall. To the west of the stepped approach another road led up parallel to it and ran direct to the south-west corner of the West Court; while yet a third branch skirted the Palace area completely and formed the highway to the Harbour Town three miles to the north.

Of the bridge which spanned the ravine, apparently changing direction twice, nothing remains but the deep foundations abutting on to the Stepped Portico; but we know that it must have joined the Viaduct to the south.

The Viaduct which stands out boldly from the south bank of the ravine was, like the Stepped Portico, laid out at the time of the first Palace (M.M. I) (Pl. IX). The piers are still preserved up to a good height. Between them are stepped culverts to allow for the passage of flood-water from the hill above. These culverts were bridged over to support the roadway, probably by means of the flat-topped corbelled arches we see in Mycenaean bridges on the mainland.

This is the most massive piece of work that has come to light in Crete. It gives a very good idea of the skill of the engineers, as well as the amount of traffic which must have run across the island from the south coast even in those early days.

The Caravanserai lies above the Viaduct. The two main rooms have been roofed over. First is a pavilion approached by a short flight of steps and fronted by a single column. A good deal of the original painted plaster remains low down on the walls, while, in its original position above, a reproduction of part of a frieze representing partridges and hoopoes has been placed (Pl. XII). Contrary to the general opinion, the many-coloured round objects at the base of the picture are not hoopoe's eggs but stones. This frieze bears considerable likeness to some of the work from the House of the Frescoes (see page 39) and the two buildings are certainly contemporaneous (M.M. III–L.M. I).

Next to the Pavilion is a stone bath for washing the feet (Pl. XIV). It was fed by pipes with water from the springs above, and flowed out into a stone drinking-trough for animals, while an emergency overflow

H

channel was also provided. The source of the water-supply has been restored.

West of the footbath is a room in which were found fragments of a number of clay bath-tubs. These, taken in conjunction with the deposit of carbonized particles in the waste-duct here, give the impression that the tired traveller could even indulge in the luxury of a hot bath.

The rest of the Caravanserai consists of small rooms and cobbled yards.

The Spring Chamber lies at an angle just to the west of the Caravanserai (Pl. XIV). Here the water in the basin wells up between the pebbles of the flooring. In the niche at the back is a lamp, while the ledges on either side were for offerings. You notice, too, the well-worn step in front of the basin. (From here to the Temple Tomb, see below.)

4 *a*. THE HOUSE OF THE HIGH PRIEST AND THE TEMPLE TOMB

From the back of the Caravanserai you climb up to the modern road and turn left along it. On the face of the cutting to the right of the road you can see, here and there, the façades of yet unexplored houses, for the whole of this hill formed part of the city of Knossos. A little farther on, just after the road has turned, there are the remains of two houses in a corn-field above, which were cleared in the first year of excavation.

Some three hundred yards from the Caravanserai is a ruined house, just below the road and to the left. Here a path leads down to a building which was partly excavated in 1931. The bulk of this house is under the road.

The House of the High Priest is so named from the stone altar which has been set back behind a chancel-like structure, a balustrade supporting two columns. On either side of the entrance are chests for offerings. Flanking the altar are stands for Double Axes, one of which is a cement copy. In front of the altar a hole leads down into a stone drain which reappears below the steps in front. The altar space seems to have been railed off by a metal grille, holes for the attachment of which can be seen between the two chests.

The east side of the house has been destroyed: only a few massive gypsum walls towards the south end have survived. The steps at this point evidently led from the paved street, which was found some way below, up to a higher thoroughfare which brought this house into direct relation with the Royal Temple Tomb.

The Royal *Temple Tomb* lies some two hundred yards on (Pl. X). After passing a house on the right of the road you ascend a steep path up the bank into a vine-yard, descending again immediately to your left down to the level of the lower entrance. This entrance leads into the north end of the Pavilion, a portico with two columns which fronts on to the open paved court. The antae of this portico have been raised to this height by the use of the original blocks which were found in a later wall. In the same way the massive pylons, on either side of the gateway facing the Pavilion, with the trident sign incised on them, have been restored by the recovery of the old blocks from elsewhere. The gypsum gateway was found complete, the lintel standing as it does at present.

To the left of the short passage that you enter now, a stairway runs up to the terrace above. The doorway into the Pillar Crypt beyond had originally a wooden lintel; this had perished and the blocks above had fallen inwards. To facilitate excavation it was therefore immediately replaced in cement. Note that the method of locking the door is the same as that employed in the South House (see page 56), while outside is a small hole to introduce a peg round which cord could be wound to seal the door from without.

The Pillar Crypt was found in an extraordinary state of preservation. The two pillars themselves were standing to their full height as was also the whole of the finely cut masonry of the lower story. Some concrete beams have had to be put in to strengthen the whole, but in the top course can easily be made out the slots to receive the rafters. The sockets for beams and rafters gave the exact method of construction. Much of the rough masonry of the upper story is also in position (see below). Shortly after its construction in M.M. III much of the tomb was destroyed by an earthquake, and stones were taken from both the Pavilion antae and the pylons and used to wall up the spaces between the pillars. In the deep enclosures thus formed were found a mass of burials; but throughout, a passage was left open to the tomb-chamber proper.

This chamber opens off the north-west corner of the Pillar Crypt. It is about twelve feet square with a square gypsum pier in the middle surrounded by the usual depressions in the gypsum paving, and lined with upright slabs of gypsum about six feet high. These slabs were held back at the corners and in the middle of each side by key slabs. These in their turn were kept in position by two huge cross-beams which ran across the central pier. The roof was originally the rough rock. It was painted a deep Egyptian blue so that the dead man lying back would, as it were, see the heavens through a square window. When the tomb chamber was excavated the beams had perished and the roof collapsed. The dampness of the soil had literally eaten away the base of the pillar and much of the lower parts of the side slabs. These, therefore, have been strengthened with cement, and a waterproof roof has been put on.

It is probable that the original coffin was of wood, with incrustations of precious metal, but at the very end of the Palace Period (L.M. II) a man, in whom we may perhaps see the last Minos of Knossos, was buried here. There is a small pit in the north-east corner and much of his funeral furniture was found. We may even have parts of his body, for in the doorway were the skull and some of the bones of a short athletic man of middle age.

The stairway, mentioned above, which runs up from the passage, leads to a terrace which runs not only over the passage but also over a space to the north. Here there is another entrance, from the north, at the higher level; and hence access was gained to the roof of the Pavilion, the way running over stone beams which span a narrow space north of the open Court.

From this terrace, also, was entered the upper story above the Pillar Crypt, much of the walls of which remain—rough stone originally plastered red. There were almost certainly two columns, corresponding to the two square piers below. The horns which stand here may have crowned the façade or have stood within. It is also possible that access to the Pillar Crypt below was obtainable by means of a trap-door, for—as the workmen said on seeing the method of locking the lower door—'dead men do not lock themselves in'.

The whole tomb bears a striking resemblance to that described by Diodorus Siculus as having been built for Minos in Sicily—a tomb below and a temple of the goddess above.

The discovery of the tomb was due to a remarkable gold ring which was found by the son of a peasant when ploughing a field some thirty yards to the south. In consequence of this chance clue, which must have been dropped by a thief, the Temple Tomb was revealed.

5. THE ROYAL TOMB AT ISOPATA

The Royal Tomb at Isopata can be approached in two ways, either by taking the path which leads up the hill after crossing the bridge about a mile from Candia and ascending the plateau of St. Nicholas, or from the Royal Villa, by going due north along the side of the Kairatos ravine for about two miles or so and then ascending up to the left. The tomb is difficult to find, being in the middle of a field surrounded by barbed wire, and the peasants do not seem to have the slightest idea of what you are talking about. But it well repays a visit, particularly if you are walking back to Candia from the Palace.

The Tomb was originally approached from the east by a long dromos which was cut in the soft rock. From this you enter a forehall, the doors at both ends of which are corbelled arches as mentioned in the Viaduct (see page 57). On either side of the forehall are niches for offerings. Set at an angle to this is the rectangular tomb-chamber some twenty-five by nineteen feet. In the north-east corner is a grave cist. In this case it is rectangular, though in the other built tomb in the district, the Tomb of the Double Axes, it is the shape of a double axe.

The roofing of the main chamber seems to have been in the nature of a corbelled vault, perhaps flat-topped like the doorways. Unfortunately the upper courses have been quarried away.

The Tomb was probably built in Late Minoan I, though it continued on in use until towards the end of the last Palace Period, Late Minoan II, when the occupant included in his funeral furniture a whole set of Egyptian alabaster vases.

A remarkable feature is a small doorway at the back of the Sepulchral Chamber, backed by the virgin soil. Both the architectural type and the openings in the walls—these in connexion with pits for libations—have received a new illustration from Professor Schaefer's discovery of the Royal Tombs in the North Syrian port of Minet-el-Beida. The Royal sepulchral type of Knossos is there taken over.

BIBLIOGRAPHY

I. General Books and Articles on Crete:

Alexiou, S.
    (1969). *Minoan Civilization* (Heraclion)
    (1973). *A Guide to the Minoan Palaces: Knossos, Phaistos, Mallia* (Heraclion)
Alexiou, and N. Platon
    (n.d.) *Guide to the Archaeological Museum at Heraclion* (Heraclion)
Alexiou, S., N. Platon, and H. Guanella.
    (1968). *Ancient Crete* (London).
Branigan, K.
    (1969). *The Foundations of Palatial Crete* (London).
Cadogan, G.
    (1976). *The Palaces of Minoan Crete* (London). An excellent survey.
Caskey, J.L.
    (1964). "Greece, Crete, and the Aegean Islands in the Early Bronze Age," *CAH* rev.ed. Vol.I, Ch. XXVI (Cambridge).
Davaras, C.
    (1976). *Guide to Cretan Antiquities* (New Jersey).
Faure, P.
    (1973). *La Vie quotidienne en Crete au temps de Minos* (Paris).
Graham, J.W.
    (1962). *The Palaces of Crète* (Princeton).
    (n.d.) *Minoan Crete* (Athens).
Higgins, R.
    (1967). *Minoan and Mycenaean Art* (New York).
    (1973). *The Archaeology of Minoan Crete* (New York).
Hood, M.S.F.
    (1967a). *Home of the Heroes: The Aegean Before the Greeks* (London).
    (1971a). *The Minoans* (London). An excellent survey of Minoan Civilization.
Hutchinson, R.
    (1962). *Prehistoric Crete* (Harmondsworth).
Huxley, G.L.
    (1961). *Crete and the Luwians* (Oxford).
Kehnscherper, G.
    (1973). *Kreta, Mykene, Santorin* (Leipzig).
Marinatos, Sp., and M. Hirmer
    (1960). *Crete and Mycenae* (New York).
    (1973). *Kreta, Thera, und das mykenische Hellas* (Munich). Excellent photographs.

Matz, F.
(1962a). *Crete and Early Greece* (London).
(1962b). "Minoan Civilization: Maturity and Zenith," *CAH* rev.ed., Vol. II, Ch. IV (b) and XII (Cambridge).

Mellersh, H.E.L.
(1967). *Minoan Crete* (New York).

Palmer, L.R.
(1961a). *Mycenaeans and Minoans* (London).

Pendlebury, J.D.S.
(1939). *The Archaeology of Crete* (New York). Still the most thorough survey of Minoan archaeology.

Platon, N.
(1966). *Crete* (London).

Renfrew, C.
(1972). *The Emergence of Civilization in the Cyclades and the Aegean in the Third Millenium B.C.* (London).

Schachermeyr, F.
(1964). *Die minoische Kultur des alten Kreta* (Stuttgart).

Shaw, J.W.
(1971). *Minoan Architecture: Materials and Techniques* (*ASAtene* 49).

Walberg, G.
(1976). *Kamares: A Study in the Character of Palatial Middle   Minoan Pottery* (*Boreas* 8) (Uppsala).

Warren, P.
(1975). *The Aegean Civilizations* (New York).

Weinberg, S.
(1965). "The Stone Age in the Aegean," *CAH* rev.ed., Vol. I, Ch. X (Cambridge).

Willetts, R.F.
(1969). *Everyday Life in Ancient Crete* (London).

Zervos, C.
(1956). *L'Art de la Crète néolithique et minoenne* (Paris). Good pictures.

Zois, A.
(1968). *Der Kamares Stil. Werden und Wesen* (Tubigen).

II. Books and Articles on Knossos:

Åstrom, P.
(1965). "Dateringen av Linear B-Tavlorna fran Knossos," *Historisk Tidskrift*, 80-93.

Betts, J.H.
(1967). "Some Unpublished Knossos Sealings and Sealstones," *BSA* 62 (1967) 27-47.

Blegen, C.W.
(1958). "A Chronological Problem," *Minoica. Zeitschrift zum 80. Geburtstag von Johannes Sundwall.* (Berlin) 61-66.

Boardman, J.
(1960). "The Knossos Tablets: An Answer," *Antiquity* 35 (1960) 233 ff.
(1962). "The Knossos Tablets Again," *Antiquity* 36 (1962) 48-51.
(1963). *The Date of the Knossos Tablets* (*On the Knossos Tablets by* L.R. Palmer and J. Boardman) (Oxford).
Boardman, J. and L.R. Palmer (1964). "The Knossos Tablets," *Antiquity* 38 (1964) 45-51.
Cadogan, G.
(1967). "Late Minoan IIIC Pottery from the Kephala Tholos Tomb near Knossos," *BSA* 62 (1967) 257-265.
Cameron, M.A.S.
(1968). "Unpublished Paintings from the 'House of the Frescoes' at Knossos," *BSA* 63 (1968) 1-33.
(1976). "Savakis's Bothros: A Minor Sounding at Knossos," *BSA* 71 (1976) 1-13.
Cameron, M.A.S., R.E. Jones, and S.E. Philippakis.
(1977) "Scientific Analyses of Minoan Fresco Samples from Knossos," *BSA* 72 (1977) 121-184.
Clark, R.J.
(1967). "The Amphorae and the Tablets of the Northern Entrance Passage at Knossos," *Pegasus* 8 (1967) 43 ff.
Evans, A.J. et.al.
(1900). "Knossos. Summary Report of the Excavation in 1900," *BSA* 6 (1899-1900) 3-92.
Evans, A.J.
(1901). "The Palace of Knossos. Provisional Report of the Excavations for the Year 1901," *BSA* 7 (1900-01) 1-120.
(1902). "The Palace of Knossos. Provisional Report of the Excavations for the Year 1902," *BSA* 8 (1901-2) 1-124.
(1903). "The Palace of Knossos. Provisional Report of the Excavations for the Year 1903," *BSA* 9 (1902-3) 1-153.
(1904). "The Palace of Knossos," *BSA* 10 (1903-4) 1-62.
(1905a). "The Palace of Knossos and its Dependencies. Provisional Report of the Year 1905," *BSA* 11 (1904-5) 1-26.
(1905b). "Prehistoric Tombs of Knossos," *Archaeologia* 49 (1905) 391-562.
(1914). "The Tomb of the Double Axes and Pillar Rooms and Ritual Vessels of the Little Palace at Knossos," *Archaeologia* 65.
(1921-36). *The Palace of Minos at Knossos* I-IV (with index volume by J. Evans). (London).
(1967). *Knossos Fresco Atlas. Catalogue of Plates* by M. Cameron and M.S.F. Hood. (Farnborough).
Evans, J.D.
(1964a). "Excavations in the Neolithic Settlement at Knossos, 1958-60, Part I," *BSA* 59 (1964) 132-241.
(1964b). "Excavations in the Neolithic Mound of Knossos, 1958-60," *Bull. Institute of Archaeology, London,* 4 (1964) 34 ff.
(1972). "The Early Minoan Occupation at Knossos. A Note to some New Evidence," *AnatSt* 22 (1972) 114 ff.

Evans, J.D., and H.N. Jarman, and N.J. Shackleton, and P. Warren.
(1968). "Knossos: Neolithic, Part II," *BSA* 63 (1968) 239-277.

Evely, D.
(1976). "A Question of Identity in the North Entrance Passage at Knossos," *BSA* 71 (1976) 57-63.

Forsdyke, E.J.
(1926-7). "The Mavro Spelio Cemetery at Knossos," *BSA* 28 (1926-7) 243-296.

Furness, A.
(1953). "The Neolithic Pottery of Knossos," *BSA* 48 (1953) 94-134.

Gill, M.
(1965), "The Knossos Sealings: Provenance and Identification," *BSA* 60 (1965) 58-99.

Graham, J.W.
(1975). "The Banquet Hall of the Little Palace," *AJA* 79 (1975) 141-5.

Hallager, E.
(1977). *The Mycenaean Palace at Knossos* (*Medalhausmuseet, Memoir* I).Stockholm.

Hawke Smith, C.H.
(1975). "The Knossos Tablets: A Reconsideration," *Kadmos* 14 (1975) 125-132.
(1976). "The Knossos Frescoes: A Revised Chronology," *BSA* 71 (1976) 65-76.

Hiller, S.
(1976). "Winejo und die 'Squatters' -überlegungen zum Knossos-problem," *Kadmos* 15 (1976) 108-129.

Hood, M.S.F.
(1952). "Late Minoan Warrior Graves from A. Ioannis and the New Hospital Site at Knossos," *BSA* 47 (1952) 243 ff.
(1956). "Another Warrior Grave at A. Ioannis near Knossos," *BSA* 51 (1956) 81 ff.
(1961). "The Date of the Linear B Tables from Knossos," *Antiquity* 35 (1961) 4-7.
(1961-2). "Chronika: Knossos," *Deltion* 17 (1961-2) Ch. 294-296.
(1962a). "Sir Arthur Evans Vindicated. A Remarkable Discovery of LM IB Vases from Beside the Royal Road at Knossos," *ILN* Feb. 17, 1962, 259-261.
(1962b). "The Knossos Tablets: A Complete View," *Antiquity* 36 (1962) 38-40.
(1963). "Stratigraphic Excavations at Knossos, 1957-61," *KrChron* 15/16 (1961-2) 92-98.
(1964). "Stratigraphy of the Linear B Tablets Found at Knossos," *MLS* 30. Sept. 1964, 299-305.
(1965a). " 'Last Palace' and 'Reoccupation' at Knossos," *Kadmos* 4 (1965) 16-44.
(1965b). "Early and Middle Minoan Periods at Knossos (Stratigraphic Excavations, 1957-1961), A Summary," *MLS* Dec. 8, 1965, 323-5.
(1966). "Date of the 'Reoccupation' Pottery from the Palace of Minos at Knossos," *Kadmos* 5 (1966) 121-41.

(1967b). "The Last Palace at Knossos and the Date of its Destruction," *SMEA* 2 (1967) 63-70.

(1968). *An Archaeological Survey of the Knossos Area.* (Oxford).

(1971b). "An Early Helladic III Import at Knossos and Anatolian Connections," *Melanges de prehistoire d'Archeocivilisation et d'ethnologie afferts a'Andre Varagnac.* (Paris).

Hooker, J.T.

(1965). "The 'Unity of the Archives' at Knossos," *Kadmos* 3 (1965) 114-121.

(1968). "The Context of the Knossos Tablets," *SMEA* 5 (1968) 71-91.

MacKenzie, D.

(1903). "The Pottery of Knossos," *JHS* 23 (1903) 157-205.

(1906). "The Middle Minoan Pottery of Knossos," *JHS* 26 (1906) 243-267.

Mellersh, H.E.L.

(1970). *The Destruction of Knossos* (London).

Palmer, L.R.

(1961b). "The Find Places of the Knossos Tablets," *Antiquity* 35 (1961) 135-141.

(1961c). "The Knossos Tablets: Some Clarifications," *Antiquity* 35 (1961) 308-311.

(1961d). "The Documentation of the Knossos Excavation," *KrChron* 15 (1961) 162-166.

(1963). *The Find Places of the Knossos Tablets (On the Knossos Tablets* by L.R. Palmer and J. Boardman) (Oxford).

(1964a). "Correspondence to the Editor," *Nestor* 2 (1964) 323-5.

(1964b). "Some New Evidence from Knossos," *MLS* 9. Dec. 1964, 306-11.

(1969a). *The Penultimate Palace at Knossos* (Rome).

(1969b). *A New Guide to the Palace at Knossos* (London).

(1971). "Mycenaean Inscribed Vases, I. The Evidence from the 'Unexplored Mansion' at Knossos," *Kadmos* 10 (1971), 70 ff.

(1972). "Mycenaean Inscribed Vases, II. The Mainland Finds," *Kadmos* 11 (1972) 27-46.

(1973). "Mycenaean Inscribed Vases, III. Consequences for Aegean History," *Kadmos* 12 (1973) 60-75.

(1974). "Knossos: Some Instructive Recent Errors," *Minos* 15 (1974) 34-67.

Palmer, L.R. and J. Raison,

(1973). "'l'Insula Nord-Ouest' du Palais de Knossos. Position des sols et stratigraphie," *Minos* 14 (1973) 17 ff.

Papin, Y.

(1978) "La Decouverte de Cnossos par Evans en 1900," *Archéologia* 116 (1978).

Pendlebury, J.D.S.

(1933). *A Guide to The Stratigraphical Museum in The Palace at Knossos.*

Pendlebury, J.D.S., and H.W. Pendlebury.

(1928-30). "Two Protopalatial Houses at Knossos," *BSA* 30 (1928-30) 53-73.

(1934). *Dating the Pottery in The Stratigraphical Museum, I.*
Pendlebury, J.D.S., E. Eccles, and M. Money-Coutts.
(1934). *Dating the Pottery in The Stratigraphical Museum.*
Pendlebury, J.D.S., and M. Money-Coutts.
(1935). *Dating the Pottery in The Stratigraphical Museum. The Plans.*
Platon, N.
(1973). "La chronologie des receptacles de tresors du sanctuaire "The Temple Repositories," et des autres depots du palais de Cnossos," *Cret Congr III, 1971.*
Popham, M.R.
(1964a). *The Last Days of the Palace at Knossos: Complete Vases of the late Minoan III B Period (SIMA 5)* (Lund).
(1964b). "The Palace at Knossos: A Matter of Definition and a Question of Fact," *AJA* 68 (1964) 349-354.
(1966a). "The Destruction of the Palace at Knossos and its Pottery," *Antiquity* 40 (1966) 24-28.
(1966b). "The Palace of Knossos. Its Destruction and Reoccupation Reconsidered," *Kadmos* 5 (1966) 17-24.
(1967). "Late Minoan Pottery: A Summary," *BSA* 62 (1967) 337-351.
(1969). "An LM III B Inscription from Knossos," *Kadmos* 8 (1969) 43ff.
(1970a). *The Destruction of the Palace at Knossos (SIMA 12)* (Goteborg).
(1970b). "A Late Minoan Shrine at Knossos," *BSA* 65 (1970) 191-5.
(1970c). "LM III B Pottery from Knossos," *BSA* 65 (1970) 195-203.
(1973). "The Unexplored Mansion at Knossos. A Preliminary Report on the Excavations from 1967-1972," *Arch Reports* 1972-3 50 ff.
(1974). "Trial KV (1969), A Middle Minoan Building at Knossos," *BSA* 69 (1974) 181-194.
(1975a). "Snakes and Ladders at Knossos. The Shifting LM Stratigraphy," *Kadmos* 13 (1975) 117-123.
(1975b). "Late Minoan II Crete: A Note," *AJA* 79 (1975) 372-374.
(1976). "An Inscribed Pithoid Jar from Knossos," *Kadmos* 15 (1976) 102-107.
(1977). "Notes from Knossos, Part I" *BSA* 72 (1977) 185-195.
Popham, M.R., + H.W. Catling
(1974). "Sellopouio Tombs 3 and 4, Two Late Minoan Graves Near Knossos," *BSA* 69 (1974) 195-258.
Raison, J.
(1963). "Une Controverse sur la Chronologie des Tablettes Cnossiennes," *Minos* 7 (1963) 151-170.
(1964). "Nouvelles discussions sur la stratigraphie cnossienne à propos d'un Livre de L.R. Palmer et J. Boardman," *REG* 77 (1964) 260-273.
(1969). *Le Grand Palais de Knossos.* (Rome).
(1977). "Le Cadmée, Knossos et le Linéaire B. A propos de plusieures ouvrages ou articles recent et d'un Livre de S. Siméonoglou," *Revue Archéologique* (1977) 79-86.

Reich, J.
(1970). "The Date of the Hieroglyphic Deposit at Knossos," *AJA* 74 (1970) 406-408.

Reusch, H.
(1958). "Zum Wandschmuck des Thronsaales in Knossos," *Minoica. Zeitschrift zum 80. Geburtstag von Johannes Sundwall.* (Berlin).
(1961). "Zum Problem des Thronraumes in Knossos," *Minoica et Homer* (ed. Georgiev Irmscher) 1961.

Vermeule, E.
(1963). "The Fall of Knossos and The Palace Style," *AJA* 67 (1963) 195-199.

Warren, P.
(1967). "A Stone Vase Maker's Workshop in the Palace at Knossos," *BSA* 62 (1967) 195-203.
(1972a). "Knossos and the Greek Mainland in the Third Millenium B.C.," *AAA* 5 (1972) 392 ff.

Woodward, W.S.
(1972). "The North Entrance at Knossos," *AJA* 76 (1972) 113-126.

Yule, P.
(1978). "On the Date of the 'Hieroglyphic Deposit ' at Knossos," *Kadmos* 17 (1978) 1-7.

III. Books and Articles on other specific sites:

Mallia

Armouretti, M.-C.
(1970). *Fouilles exécutées a Mallia. Le Centre Politique II. La Crypte Hypostyle (1957-1963) Études Cretoises* 18 (Paris).

Chapouthier, F., and J. Charbonneaux
(1928). *Fouilles exécutées a Mallia. Premier Rapport (1922-24) Études Cretoises* 1 (Paris)

Chapouthier, F., and R. Joly
(1936). *Fouilles exécutées a Mallia. Deuxieme Rapport. Explorations du Palais (1925-6). Études Cretoises* 4 (Paris)

Chapouthier, F., and P. Demargne
(1942). *Fouilles exécutées a Mallia. Troisiéme Rapport. Explorations du Palais. Études Cretoises* 6 (Paris)

Demargne, P.
(1945). Fouilles exécutées a Mallia. Exploration des necropoles (1921-33). Premier fascicule. *Etudes Cretoises* 7 (Paris).
(1953). *Fouilles exécutées a Mallia. Explorations des maisons et quartiers d'habitation (1921-48). Premier fascicule. Études Cretoises* 9 (Paris).

Deshayes, J. et.al.
(1958). *Fouilles exécutées a Mallia. Explorations des maisons et quartiers d'habitation. Deuxieme fascicule. Études Cretoises* 11 (Paris).

van Effenterre, H. and M.
(1963). *Fouilles exécutées a Mallia. Étude du site et explorations des necropoles (1915-1928). Études Cretoises* 13 (Paris).
(1969). *Fouilles exécutées a Mallia. Le centre politique I. L'Agora (1960-66). Études Cretoises* 17 (Paris).
(1976). *Fouilles exécutées a Mallia. Exploration des maisons et quartiers d'habitation (1956-1960). Quatrieme fasicule. Études Cretoises* 22 (Paris)

Pelon, O.
(1970). *Fouilles exécutées a Mallia. Exploration des maisons et quartiers d'habitation (1963-66). Premier fascicule. Études Cretoises* 7 (Paris).

Phaistos

Levi, D.
(1960), "Per una nuova classificazione della Civiltà Minoica." *La Parola del Pasato* 71 (1960) 81-121.
(1964). *The Recent Excavations at Phaistos, (SIMA* 11) (Lund).
(1976). *Festos e la civiltà minoica.* (Rome).

Pernier, L. and L. Banti
(1935). *Il Palazzo Minoico di Festos, I. Gil Strati piu Antichi e il Primo Plazzo.* (Rome).
(1951). *Il Palazzo Minoico di Festos, II. Il Secondo Palazzo* (Rome).

Zakro

Platon, N.
(1967). *Praktika,* 162 ff.
(1968). *Praktika,* 149 ff.
(1969). *Praktika,* 197 ff.
(1970). *Praktika,* 208 ff.
(1971a). *Praktika,* 231 ff.
(1971b). *Zakros, The Discovery of a Lost Palace of Ancient Crete* (New York).

Katsamba

Alexiou, S.
(1953). "Anaskaphai en Katsamba," *Praktika* 1953, 299-308.

Lebena

Alexiou, S.
(1958). "Ein Frühminoisches Grab bei Lebena," *AA* 1958, 1 ff.
(1960). "Lebena," *BCH* 84 (1960) 844 ff.
(1963). "Oi Protominoikoi Taphoi tis Lebenas kai i Exelixis ton Protominoikon Rhythmon," *KrChron* 15/16 (1961-2) 88-91.

Myrtos

Warren, P.
>(1972). *Myrtos: An Early Bronze Age Settlement in Crete* (*BSA Supplement 7*) (Oxford).

(All abbreviations are taken from "Notes to Contributors" in the *American Journal of Archaeology* Volume 82, pp. 1-8.
Exception: MLS = Minutes of the Mycenaean Siminar, Institute of Classical Studies, University of London).

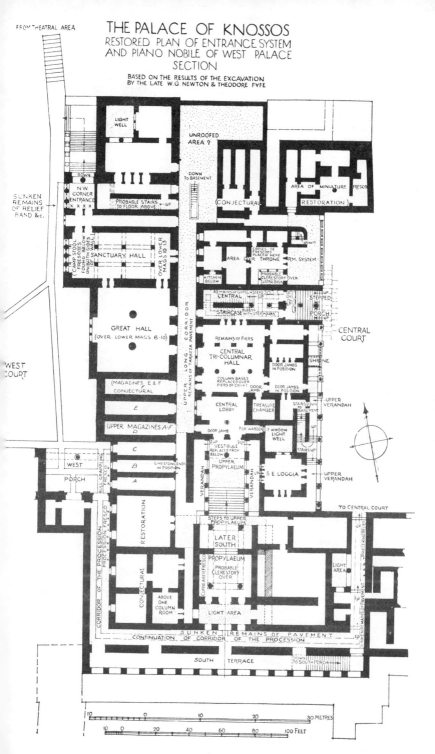

THE PALACE OF KNOSSOS
RESTORED PLAN OF ENTRANCE SYSTEM AND PIANO NOBILE OF WEST PALACE SECTION

BASED ON THE RESULTS OF THE EXCAVATION
BY THE LATE W.G. NEWTON & THEODORE FYFE

FROM THEATRAL AREA

LIGHT WELL

UNROOFED AREA ?

DOWN to Basement

(CONJECTURAL)

AREA OF MINIATURE FRESCO (RESTORATION)

SUNKEN REMAINS OF RELIEF BAND &c.

DOWN

N.W. CORNER ENTRANCE XXXX

PROBABLE STAIRS TO FLOOR ABOVE — UP

COPIES OF FRESCOES PLACED HERE

 M. SYSTEM

CAMP STOOL FRESCOES FRIEZE BELOW ON BOTH SIDES

SANCTUARY HALL

OVER LOWER MAGS 10-13

AREA OVER THRONE

KITCHEN BELOW

PROBABLE CLERESTORY OVER LUSTRAL BASIN

REMAINS OF GYPSUM STEPS TO

CENTRAL STAIRCASE BURNT WITH STEP MARKS

GREAT HALL (OVER LOWER MAGS 6-10)

REMAINS OF PIERS

CENTRAL TRI-COLUMNAR HALL

COLUMN BASES REPLACED OVER PIERS OF CRYPT

DOOR JAMBS IN POSITION

DOOR JAMBS IN POSITION

DOOR JAMB

SHRINE

(MAGAZINES E & F CONJECTURAL)

E

CENTRAL LOBBY

TREASURE CHAMBER

STAIRS DOWN TO BASEMENT

UPPER VERANDAH

UPPER MAGAZINES A-F

D

DOOR JAMB

FOR WARDER

? WINDOW

LIGHT WELL

STAIRS UP

WEST COURT

WEST PORCH

C

B

A

LIMESTONE ENDS IN POSITION

UP

VESTIBULE REPLACED FROM BELOW

UPPER PROPYLAEUM

BULL GRAPPLING FRESCO

UPPER LONG CORRIDOR — REMAINS OF TARAZZA PAVEMENT

VERANDAH

VERANDAH

S.E. LOGGIA

UPPER VERANDAH

TO CENTRAL COURT

CENTRAL COURT

STEPPED PORCH UP

UP

UP

RESTORATION

CONJECTURAL

ABOVE ONE COLUMN ROOM

STEPS TO UPPER PROPYLAEUM

LATER SOUTH PROPYLAEUM

PROBABLE CLERESTORY OVER

LIGHT AREA

LIGHT AREA

UPPER AREA FRESCO

CORRIDOR OF THE PROCESSION FRESCO

SUNKEN REMAINS OF PAVEMENT

CONTINUATION OF CORRIDOR OF THE PROCESSION

DOWN TO SOUTH PORCH

SOUTH TERRACE

PORTICO & REMAINS OF PAVEMENT

10   0   10   20   30 METRES

10   0   20   40   60   80   100 FEET

PLAN No. 3

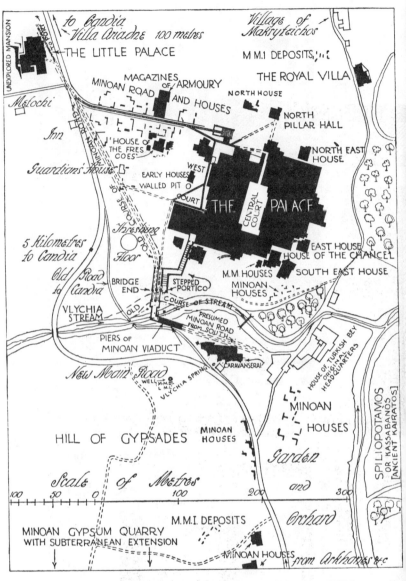

PLAN No. 4. PLAN OF PALACE AND SURROUNDINGS

PLAN No. 6. PLAN OF ROYAL VILLA

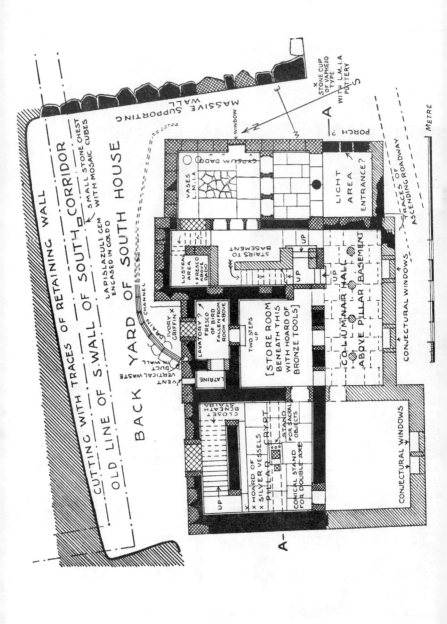

CUTTING WITH TRACES OF RETAINING WALL

OLD LINE OF S. WALL OF SOUTH CORRIDOR

SMALL STONE CHEST WITH MOSAIC CUBES

LAPIS LAZULI GEM ENCASED IN GOLD

BACK YARD OF SOUTH HOUSE

MASSIVE SUPPORTING WALL

STONE CUP OF VAPHEIO TYPE

WITH L.M.I.A POTTERY

A

PORCH ?

WINDOW

GYPSUM DADO

VASES L.M.I.A

LIGHT AREA ENTRANCE ?

TRACES OF ASCENDING ROADWAY

CONJECTURAL WINDOWS

METRE

DRAIN CHANNEL

IVORY GRIFFIN

VERTICAL WASTE DUCT IN WALL

VENT

LUSTRAL AREA

FRESCO DADO

STAIRS TO BASEMENT

UP

UP

UP

LAVATORY ?

FRESCO FALLEN FROM ROOM ABOVE

LATRINE

TWO STEPS UP

[STORE ROOM BENEATH THIS WITH HOARD OF BRONZE TOOLS]

COLUMNAR HALL ABOVE PILLAR BASEMENT

CLOSET BENEATH STAIRS

HOARD OF SILVER VESSELS

PILLAR CRYPT

STAND FOR SACRAL OBJECTS

CONICAL STAND FOR DOUBLE-AXE

UP

CONJECTURAL WINDOWS

A

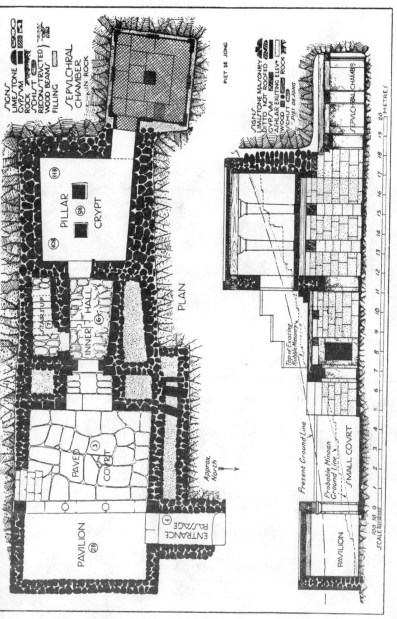

PLAN No. 8.   THE BASEMENT PLAN AND SECTIONAL PLAN OF THE TEMPLE TOMB

PLATE I

1. *GENERAL VIEW FROM THE SOUTH*

2. *WEST COURT*

PLATE II

2. *MAGAZINES*

1. *SOUTH PROPYLAEUM*

PLATE III

1. THEATRAL AREA

2. GRAND STAIRCASE

PLATE IV

2. *DOUBLE-AXE PILLAR*

1. *NORTH ENTRANCE*

PRIEST-KING FRESCO

PLATE VI

1. *QUEEN'S MEGARON*

2. *HALL OF THE DOUBLE AXES RESTORED*

PLATE VII

1. *GIANT PITHOI*

2. *SHRINE OF THE DOUBLE AXES*

PLATE VIII

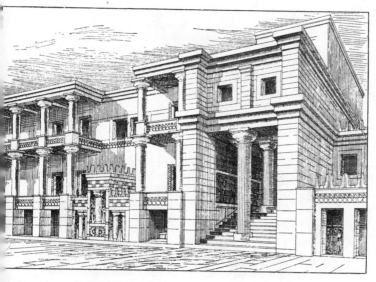

1. RESTORED VIEW OF W. PALACE WING

2. LITTLE PALACE

PLATE IX

1. *SOUTH HOUSE*

2. *VIADUCT*

PLATE X

1. *CARAVANSERAI AND VIADUCT FROM THE PALACE*

2. *TEMPLE TOMB*

PLATE XI

PLATE XII

PARTRIDGE AND HOOPOE FRESCO

PLATE XII.

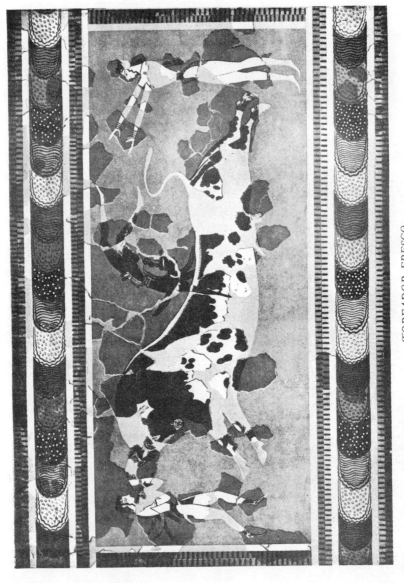

TOREADOR FRESCO

PLATE XIV

1. *FOOTBATH IN THE CARAVANSERAI*

2. *SPRING CHAMBER*

L.C. REILLY

SLAVES
IN
ANCIENT
GREECE

SLAVES FROM GREEK

MANUMISSION INSCRIPTIONS

SLAVES IN ANCIENT GREECE: A Prosopography from the Manumission Inscriptions.
Linda Collins Reilly
ISBN 0-89005-223-9. 200 pp. *$25.00*

The first complete attempt to form a prosopography of Greek slaves known from manumission inscriptions. This new work is for the first time published by ARES PUBLISHERS as a part of the program for the encouragement of studies in Greek Epigraphy and Prosopography.

This new prosopography is valuable not only because it establishes for the user how common were some of the slave-names but also it gives a realistic picture about how little we know about slaves and slavery in the Greek World.

ANCIENT
GREEK
NUMERICAL
systems

By

MARCVS NIEBVHR TOD

WITH A PREFATORY NOTE
BY
JOSEPH BRESLIN

No Classical or historical Bibliography had an entry until now for a book examining the *Ancient Greek Numerical Systems*. Epigraphical handbooks and introductory works, when they had to refer to this subject listed the articles published by Marcus Niebuhr Tod from 1911 to 1954. The availability of those articles, however, was another problem. No scholar could possibility have in his personal library the needed volumes from the *BSA* and the *JHS* and many institutional libraries are of no help because they have incomplete sets of both journals.

ARES decided to cover this bibliographical gap. All that Tod has written and published on Greek Numerical Systems, has been carefully collected by Mr. J. Breslin in this volume, which we hope will be considered soon as a very valuable and unique reference to be added to every scholar's and educational institution's library.

vii + 105 pp. $20

ARES PUBLISHERS Inc.
612 NORTH MICHIGAN AVE . SUITE 216
CHICAGO, ILLINOIS 60611

REVERSE-LEXICON OF GREEK PROPER-NAMES

Rückläufiges Wörterbuch der Griechischen Eigennamen

F. DORNSEIFF & BERNARD HANSEN

ISBN 0-89005-251-4.   xvi + 340 pp. $25.00

Hardbound and Goldstamped

With this reprint edition of the extremely rare *Reverse Lexicon of Greek Proper Names*, ARES offers one more valuable service to Classical scholarship. Dornseiff-Hansen, a reference previously available only through inter-library loan, is now available to every scholar and library.

The reprint edition is actually more useful to the English speaking scholars than the original. The *Preface* and the *Remarks* of the compilers appear in English translation, a brief bibliography (1954-1978) has been added, and as special appendix, Prof. L. Zgusta's reverse index of the indigenous names of Asia Minor is also included.

Dornseiff-Hansen is actually the best available Lexicon for the Greek Proper-Names. It includes all the names from Pape-Benseler, Preisigke's *Namenbuch*, and hundreds of NEW names from papyri and inscriptions discovered from 1922 until the year 1954.

PROCOPE S. COSTAS

AN OUTLINE OF THE HISTORY
OF THE
GREEK LANGUAGE

WITH PARTICULAR EMPHASIS ON THE
KOINE AND THE SUBSEQUENT PERIODS

ISBN 0-89005.   xxvi + 143pp. $15.00

Selecting a very modest title for his book, Prof. Dr. P.S. Costas (1900-1974) called his history of the Greek Language an *Outline* and then added in the subtitle: *With Particular Emphasis on the Koine and Subsequent Periods.*

The original edition of the book (Chicago 1936) had all the possible mis-adventures that a scholarly book can have upon its publication. Very few copies were sent for review and no copies reached the booksellers and distributors, because most of the edition was destroyed in a Chicago warehouse.

Costas wrote his book encouraged by Paul Shorey and under the *aegis* of Carl Darling Buck and Walter Petersen at the University of Chicago. It is actually the best scholarly history of the Greek Language, contains excellent bibliography and uses a great number of references on subjects rarely mentioned in the other histories. A *must* for every classical scholar and an absolute necessity for the reference section of every library.

ALEXANDER THE GREAT CHARGING THE BODYGUARD AND OFFICERS OF THE PERSIAN
KING AT THE BATTLE OF ISSUS

ALEXANDER THE GREAT
AND THE HELLENISTIC WORLD
Macedonian Imperialism and the
Hellenization of the East.

By
PIERRE JOUGUET

*Sometime Member of the French School at Athens, Professor at
the University of Paris, Correspondent of the Institute of France*

Starting with Alexander's campaign against the Persian Empire, the
author proceeds to the establishment of the Empire of Asia, which, after the
Indian campaign, was transformed to a world empire. Jouguet examines
carefully the character of the Macedonian hegemony, its administrative
ability and the new Greek cities which sprang up in the new territories. The
dismemberment of the Empire after Alexander's death, and the rivalry of
the powers, precede the examination of the Hellenistic world with emphasis
on the Hellenisation of Egypt and the birth of the Graeco-Oriental
kingdoms. An outstanding historical reference work absoutely necessary for
every educational or public library. Extensive bibliography, notes. Many
maps.

ISBN 0-89005-256-5. Two volumes bound in one. xx + 231 + iv and
vii + [233-]440. $25.00

ATHLETICS
OF THE
ANCIENT WORLD

By

E. NORMAN GARDINER, D.Litt.

**With a Preface to the American Edition
By
PROF. STEPHEN G. MILLER
University of California
at Berkeley.**

ISBN 0-89005-257-3.   xviii + 246pp + 64pl. $22.00

"Nearly half a century has passed since the original appearance of E. Norman Gardiner's *Athletics of the Ancient World*. In the interval many discoveries have been made which ought to have rendered Gardiner's work obsolete; many books have been written on the subject which ought to have replaced *Athletics of the Ancient World*. It has, however, not been replaced as is shown not only by this, but also by previous reprints in 1955, 1965, 1967, and 1971, all of which have sold out making the book once more unavailable. The principal reason for the continued usefulness of *AAW* lies with its author. E. Norman Gardiner was recognized during his own lifetime as the unrivaled authority on Greek Athletics...

....The timelessness of Gardiner's work lies, then, partly in his enormous learning. It lies even more, however, in his ability to write intelligibly for both the interested layman and the specialized scholar. The status of our knowledge is made clear, the source of information obvious, problems well defined, but never to the confusion of the reader. His learning sits gracefully upon his lucid prose, and one recognizes that Gardiner knew his subject matter intimately, cared for it tremendously, and wanted to share it generously."

From the *Preface* by Prof. Stephen Miller.

T.A. BRADY

SARAPIS & ISIS

COLLECTED ESSAYS

viii + 130 pp. 8 ½ x 11 inch. ISBN 0-089005-253-0 $25.00

For every scholar who is presently engaged in the study of the Near-Eastern religions and the influence of Egyptian and Syrian cults on Hellenistic and Roman paganism, the "Brady papers" from the cornerstone on which should be based any study of Sarapis and Isis.

Thomas Allan Brady (1902-1964) started working on Sarapis and Isis first under the direction of W.S. Ferguson and A.D. Nock at Harvard. His monograph, *The Reception of the Egyptian Cults by the Greeks 330-30 B.C.* (1935), made him internationally known as an authority on this subject. A few years later, Brady collected all the known monuments about those cults in his equally famous *Repertory of Statuary and Figured Monuments Related to the Cults of the Egyptian Gods* (1938) which was issued in a very limited mimeograph edition, but was never printed or officially published until now.

The last "Brady paper" on *"A Head of Sarapis from Corinth"* was published in 1941. It holds still a prominent place in all the bibliographies on Hellenistic Art and Sarapis.

Prof. Fordyce Mitchell recommended that the three "Brady papers" should form a single volume, providing thus a work much needed for reference by scholars and libraries.

ARES was very happy to translate Prof. Mitchell's recommendation into reality by publishing this extremely valuable book in order to make it available for the first time to scholars and libraries.

THE FRAGMENTS
OF THE LOST HISTORIANS
OF ALEXANDER THE GREAT

Fragmenta Scriptorum de Rebus Alexandri Magni, Pseudo-Callisthenes itinerarium Alexandri.

GREEK TEXT AND FACING LATIN
TRANSLATION WITH INTRODUCTIONS
AND COMMENTARIES IN LATIN

EDITED BY
KARL MÜLLER

xvi + 162 + xxxii + 180 pp. (Total 390 pp. 6 x 9 inch) $30.00

This essential reference work needed by every scholar who studies the campaigns and the history of the empire formed by Alexander the great, was originally published in Paris the year 1846. It was never known as an independent work, but as part of Dubner's edition of *Arrian* in the series of Greek and Latin writers published by Firmin Didot.

Since Dubner's *Arrian* was bypassed as a reference edition by the one of A.G. Roos (*Arrianus*, vol. I, Leipzig/Teubner 1907), many libraries discarded the older edition unintentionally discarding also Müller's *SRAM* which was bound with it. When librarians and scholars became aware that this discarding was a big mistake it was too late. The 'discards' were already sold and no way existed to replace the lost reference work.

By issuing the first independent edition of Müller's *SRAM*, ARES gives the opportunity to the younger generations of scholars and institutional libraries to add to their reference shelves this valuable work. We hope also that librarians of older institutional libraries will grasp this opportunity to add again to their collections a much needed work that may have been discarded by mistake in the past.

ARES PUBLISHERS Inc.
612 NORTH MICHIGAN AVE., SUITE 216
CHICAGO, ILLINOIS 60611

THE ARES SERIES OF ANCIENT & MEDIAEVAL GREEK AND ROMAN WRITERS

"AUTHORS AND WORKS NOT IN THE LOEB LIBRARY"

ISIDOR OF CHARAX, PARTHIAN STATIONS. Greek text with facing English Translation, Commentary and Notes by *W.H. Schoff*. 60 pp. ISBN 0-89005-058-9 **$10.00**

HANNO THE CARTHAGINIAN, PERIPLUS. Greek text with facing English Translation, Commentary, Notes and facsimile of Codex Palatinus Gr. 398 by *Al. N. Oikonomides*, with Extracts from *W.H. Schoff, E.A. Bunbury* and the complete edition by *F. Kluge* (1829) as Appendix. 56 + 50 pp. ISBN 0-89005-217-4 **$10.00**

THEOPHRASTUS, METAPHYSICS. Greek text with facing English Translation, Commentary and Introduction by *W.D. Ross* and *F.H. Fobes.* xxxii + 87 pp. ISBN 0-89005-254-9 **$10.00**

MARINOS OF NEAPOLIS, The EXTANT WORKS or THE LIFE OF PROCLUS and THE COMMENTARY ON THE DEDOMENA OF EUCLID. Greek text with facing English Translation. *Testimonia de Vita Marini*. Introduction and Notes by *Al. N. Oikonomides.* 107 pp. ISBN 0-89005-218-12 **$15.00**

RUFUS FESTUS AVIENUS, ORA MARITIMA or DESCRIPTION OF THE SEA-COAST (FROM BRITTANY ROUND TO MASSILIA). Latin text with facing English Translation, Commentary, Notes and Facsimile of ISBN 0-89005-175-5. **$10.00**

CRATERUS, THE FRAGMENTS FROM HIS COLLECTION OF ATHENIAN DECREES: De Crateri Psephismaton Synagoge et de Locis Aliquot Plutarchi ex ea Petitis. Edidit *Paulus Krech* (Greek text with Latin Commentary). 106 pp. ISBN 0-89005-208-5. **$10.00**

POLYAENUS, THE STRATAGEMS OF WAR. English Translation only by *R. Shepherd*. 408 pp. ISBN 0-89005-020-1 **$15.00**

PLINY THE ELDER, *THE CHAPTERS ON THE HISTORY OF ART*. Latin Text with facing English Translation, Commentary and Notes by *K. Jex-Blake* and *E. Sellers*. With New Bibliographical Sections up to 1975 by *R.V. Schoder*. 252 pp. ISBN 0-89005-055-4. **$15.00**

EPIGRAMMATA, INSCRIPTIONS GRAECAE METRICAE EX SCRIPTORIBUS PRAETER ANTHOLOGIAM COLLECTAE. Greek text with Latin Commentary by *Th. Preger.* xxviii + 252 pp. ISBN 0-89005-214-X **$25.00**

LYRICA, MEDIAEVAL GREEK TEXTS. A Collection of the Earliest Compositions in Vulgar Greek prior to the Year 1500. Greek texts with English Commentaries and Notes by *W. Wagner.* xxxiv + 192 pp. ISBN 0-89005-211-5. **$10.00**

OPERA SELECTA
OF OUR CENTURY'S
CLASSICAL SCHOLARS

NEW BOOKS: WINTER
1979/1980

CORNFORD, F.M., *MICROCOSMOGRAPHIA ACADEMICA,* ISBN
0-89005-318-9, 64 pp. **$3.00**

DODDS, E.R., *SELECT PASSAGES ILLUSTRATING NEOPLATONISM,*
ISBN 0-89005-302-2. 128 pp. **$12.50**

KAPSOMENAKIS, SG., *VORUNTERSUCHUNGEN ZU EINER
GRAMMATIK DER PAPYRI DER NACHCHRISTLICHEN ZEIT,*
ISBN 0-89005-294-8. xvi + 148 pp. **$12.50**

TOD, M.N., *EPIGRAPHICAL NOTES ON GREEK COINAGE,*
ISBN 0-89005-319-7, 116 pp. (includes a bibliography of all of
Tod's works). **$15.00**

ARANGIO-RUIZ, V. & OLIVIERI, A., *INSCRIPTIONES GRAECAE
SICILIAE ET INFIMAE ITALIAE AD IUS PERTINENTES,* ISBN
0-89005-321-9. xi + 289 pp. **$25.00**

BRUNCO, G.& STANJEK, J, *DEMETRIUS OF PHALERUM, DICTA
SEPTEM SAPIENTUM, THE COMMANDMENTS OF THE SEVEN
WISE MEN.*ISBN 0-89005-322-7. xvi + 146 pp. **$20.00**

WILAMOWITZ-MOELLENDORFF, U., *GREEK HISTORICAL WRITING
AND APOLLO,* translated by *Gilbert Murray.* ISBN 0-89005-320-0,
46 pp. **$4.00**

ORDER DIRECTLY FROM ARES FOR SPEEDIEST DELIVERY!

ARES PUBLISHERS Inc.
612 NORTH MICHIGAN AVE., SUITE 216
CHICAGO, ILLINOIS 60611

NEW BOOKS
FALL 1979

BEES, N., ED. *CHRONICON MONEMBASIAE.* A Study of its sources and its value as a historical source; Accompanied by a criticcal edition of its three versions of the Greek text printed in parallel columns. With an Introduction to the American Edition by Al. N. Oikonomides. ISBN 0-89005-279-4, pp. xvi + 50 ....**$12.50**

BOYLAN, P., *THOTH—THE HERMES OF EGYPT.* ISBN 0-89005-280-8, pp. ix + 215 ....**$12.50**

BUDGE, WALLIS, E.A., *CLEOPATRA'S NEEDLES AND OTHER EGYPTIAN OBELISKS.* ISBN 0-89005-278-6, pp. xvi + 308 + 17 plates **$20.00**

COEDES, G., *TESTIMONIA OF GREEK AND LATIN WRITERS ON THE LANDS AND PEOPLES OF THE FAR EAST.* 4th C. B.C. to 14th C. A.D. ISBN 0-89005-289-1, xii + 188 (in French). **$20.00**

COOKE, H.P., *OSIRIS, A STUDY IN MYTHS, MYSTERIES AND RELIGION.* ISBN 0-89005-287-5, pp. 159. ....**$12.50**

CURTIS, J.E., *THE COINAGE OF PHARAONIC EGYPT.* ISBN 0-89005-283-2. Paperback....................................**$3.00**

DE MORGAN, J., *MANUEL DE NUMISMATIQUE ORIENTALE DE L'ANTIQUITE ET DU MOYEN-AGE.* vi + 480 pp. Profusely illustrated.
Hardbound ISBN 0-89005-308-1 ....**$30.00**
Softbound ISBN 0-89005-296-4 ....**$20.00**

DE ROUGE, J., F., FEUARDENT. *THE COINAGES OF THE NOMES & PREFECTURES OF ROMAN EGYPT.* (in French). 121 pp. Illustrated.
Hardbound ISBN 0-89005-315-4 ....**$20.00**
Softbound ISBN 0-89005-314-6 ....**$10.00**

DESSAU, HERMANN, *INSCRIPTIONES LATINAE SELECTAE.* ISBN 0-89005-274-3. The Set of Five Volumes, pp. 2,845. Papercovers **$125.00**

DUNBABIN, T.J., *THE WESTERN GREEKS,* ISBN 0-89005-300-6, xvi + 504 pp. **$30.00**

DUNBABIN, T.J., *THE GREEKS AND THEIR EASTERN NEIGHBOURS,* ISBN 0-89005-317-0, 96 pp. + 17 plates. **$15.00**

EDELSTEIN, L., *THE HIPPOCRATIC OATH.* ISBN 0-89005-272-7, pp. vii + 90 ....**$10.00**

GREGOIRE, H., *RECUEIL DES INSCRIPTIONS GRECQUES-CHRETIENNES D'ASIE MINEURE.* ISBN 0-89005-291-3, pp. vii + 128 ....**$20.00**

GROSE, S.W., *CATALOGUE OF THE McCLEAN COLLECTION OF GREEK COINS. [IN THE FITZWILLIAM MUSEUM, CAMBRIDGE].*
    VOL. I. *Western Europe, Magna Graecia, Sicily.* xii + 380 pp. + 111 plates.
    VOL. II. *Greek Mainland, Aegean Islands, Crete,* vi + 564 pp. + 137 plates.
    VOL. III. *Asia Minor, Further Asia, Egypt, Africa.* vi + 508 pp. + 132 plates.
    ISBN 0-89005-305-7, 1,476 pp. + 380 plates. (Large 7 x 10 inch format)   Hardbound **$195.00**

HEAD, B.V., *ON THE CHRONOLOGICAL SEQUENCE OF THE COINS OF EPHESUS.* ISBN 0-89005-306-5. vi + 89 pp. + 5 plates. Hardbound **$20.00**

ICARD, S., *DICTIONARY OF GREEK COIN INSCRIPTIONS.* xxiv + 563 pp.
    Hardbound ISBN 0-89005-307-3 . . . .**$30.00**
    Softbound   ISBN 0-89005-295-6 . . . .**$20.00**

JONES, W.H.S., *PHILOSOPHY AND MEDICINE IN ANCIENT GREECE.* ISBN 0-89005-286-7, pp. 100 . . . .**$10.00**

KAN, A.H., *JUPPITER DOLICHENUS,* Sammlung der Inschriften und Bildwerke. ISBN 0-89005-285-9, x + 156 + 16 plates. **$15.00**

KANATZOULIS, D., *PROSOPOGRAPHIA MACEDONICA, From 148 B.C. until the time of Constantine the Great.* ISBN 0-89005-316-2, xvi + 190 pp. **$20.00**

LAMBROS, S.P., *ECTHESIS CHRONICA AND CHRONICON ATHENARUM.* ISBN 0-89005-284-0 . . . .**$12.50**

MALLET, M. DOMINIQUE, *LES RAPPORTS DES GRECS AVEC L'EGYPT.* (Relations of the Ancient Greeks with late Pharaonic and Persian Egypt. From the Conquest by Cambyses to Alexander the Great 521-331 B.C.). ISBN 0-89005-299-9. vii + 218 pp. **$30.00**

McCLEAN, J.R., *THE ORIGIN OF WEIGHT.* ISBN 0-89005-304-9, 61 pp. Papercover. **$5.00**

MILLER, STEPHEN, ED., *ARETE,* Ancient writers, papyri, and inscriptions on the history and ideals of Greek athletics an games. ISBN 0-89005-313-8. Paperback. **$7.50**

MULLER, K., *THE FRAGMENTS OF THE LOST HISTORIANS OF ALEXANDER THE GREAT.* ISBN 0-89005-273-5. pp. vi + 162 + xxxii + 180 . . . .**$30.00**

O'LEARY DE LACY, *HOW THE GREEK SCIENCE PASSED TO THE ARABS.* ISBN 0-89005-282-4, vi + 196 pp. **$12.50**

PENDLEBURY, J.D.S., *A HANDBOOK TO THE PALACE OF MINOS AT KNOSSOS.* With an Introduction and Bibliography by Leslie Preston Day. ISBN 0-89005-312-X. Paperback. **$8.50**

RAVEL, O.E., *LES "POULAINS" DE CORINTHE.* ISBN 0-89005-309-X. 448 pp. + 78 plats. (6 x 9 inch format) **$50.00**

ROBINSON, E.S.G., *SYLLOGE NUMMORUM GRAECORUM. THE LLOYD COLLECTION. BRITISH SERIES, VOL. II.* ISBN 0-89005-310-3 59 pp. + 59 plates. 4 Fascicules hardbound in one. (Large 11 x 15½ inch format). **$95.00**

ARES PUBLISHERS Inc.

612 NORTH MICHIGAN AVE., SUITE 216
CHICAGO, ILLINOIS 60611

THE
ANCIENT WORLD

A NEW SCHOLARLY JOURNAL DEDICATED TO STUDY OF THE WORLD OF THE ANCIENTS.

Volume I, 1978 (Issues 1, 2, 3, 4 available)
Volume II, 1979 (Issues 1, 2, available. Issues (3, 4, In preparation)

WE KEEP UP PUBLISHING DATES,WE SELECT THE BEST ARTICLES, EVERY MANUSCRIPT SUBMITTED TO US HAS PROMPT AND UNBIASED ATTENTION.WE TRY TO DELIVER TO OUR SUBSCRIBERS A JOURNAL THAT PUBLISHES NEW TEXTS, NEW INTERPRETATIONS AND NEW RESEARCH.

Our subscription is the same as when we started. $10.00 per year (4 issues). If you are not already a subscriber $20.00 will bring to you all the issues published to date, plus the two issues presently in press (*AW* II, 1979, No, 3, 4.). $30.00, will make sure that you will get four more issues in 1980 (*AW* III, 1980, Nos 1,2,3,4,.), AT THE SAME SUBSCRIPTION PRICE.

SETS OF REFERENCE WORKS FROM
ARES

INSCRIPTIONES LATINAE SELECTAE
ED. HERMANN DESSAU
JUST OFF THE PRESS AUGUST 1979

ISBN 0-89005-274-3. Five Volumes, 2,845 pp. Paper Covers. . . **$125.00**
An outstanding collection of Latin Inscriptions from every corner of the
Roman World with excellent commentaries and *most importantly*
copiously indexed.
This set of five volumes is sold elsewhere at about U.S. $250-275.
Compare Ares price and purchase a set for your personal library.

**INSCRIPTIONES ATTICAE (INSCRIPTIONES GRAECAE, EDITION
   MINOR)** Ed. Johannes Kirchner and Friedrich Hiller von Gaertringen.
Vol.   1: IG I . *Inscriptiones Attice Eulidis Anno Anteriores.*
   Ed. F. Hiller de Gaertringen.
Vol. 2: IG II . *Inscriptiones Atticae Euclidis Anno Posteriores.*
   Ed. I. Kirchner (1-1369).
Vol. 3: IG II . *Inscriptiones Atticae Euclidis Anno Posteriores.* Ed. I.
   Kirchner (2788-5219). vii, 362 pp., Indices, Archontum Tabulae,
   Chronologica, Sermo Publicus Decretorum Proprius. 68 pp.
Vol. 5: IG: II . *Inscriptiones Atticae Euclidis Anno Posteriores.* Ed. I.
   Kirchner (5220-13247).
The Set of Five Volumes: ISBN 0-89005-013-9 . . . . **$125.00**
This set has been called the ''best bargain in the scholarly world.''
It still is, and at the same price as it was in 1974.

SUPPLEMENTUM INSCRIPTIONUM ATTICARUM I, IG I^{2}, II^{2}/III^{2}
   Paraleipomena et Addenda. Ed. Al. N. Oikonomides, ISBN 0-89005-
   126-7, pp. x + 504 + 34 + 68. . . . . **$25.00**
SUPPLEMENTUM INSCRIPTIONUM ATTICARUM II, IG I^{2}, II^{2}/III^{2}
   Paraleipomena et Addenda. Ed. Al. N. Oikonomides, ISBN 0-89005-
   249-2, pp. xvi + 300 . . . . **$25.00**
SUPPLEMENTUM INSCRIPTIONUM ATTICARUM III, IG I^{3}, II^{2}/III^{2}
   Paraleipomena et Addenda, Ed. Al. N. Oikonomides, ISBN 0-89005-
   275-1 . . . . **$25.00**
SUPPLEMENTUM INSCRIPTIONUM ATTICARUM IV, IG I^{2}, II^{2}/III^{2}
   Paraleipomena et Addenda. Ed. Al. N. Oikonomides—Forthcoming
   Fall 1979/80.

INSCRIPTIONES GRAECAE AD RES ROMANAS PETRINENTES.
ED. R. CAGNAT, J. TOUTAIN, P. JOUGUET, ET G. LAFAYE.
Vol. I: (et II): *Inscriptiones Europae [Praeter Graeciam]* Africae Britan-
niae, Germaniae, Galliae, Hispaniae, Italiae, Siciliae, Sardiniae,
Melitae, Pannoniae, Daciae, Dalmatiae, Thraciae, Mosesiae,
Superioris et Inferioris, Sarmatiae, Bospori, Mauretaniae,
Numidiae, Africae, Cretae, Cyrenaicae, Aegypti. (R 1911)
Vol. III: *Inscriptiones Asiae I.* Bithyniae, Ponti, Cappadociae, Armeniae
Majoris, Galatiae, Lyciae, Pamphyliae, Ciliciae, Cyrpi, Syriae,
Palaestinae, Arabiae. (R 1906)
Vol. IV: *Inscriptiones Asiae II:* Tenedi, Lesbi, Proconnesi, Besbici,
Mysiae, Phrygiae, Chii, Sami, Amorgi, Calymnae, Astypalaeae,
Coi, Nisyri, Symes, Chalces, Rhodi, Carpathi, Lydiae. (R 1927)
ISBN 0-89005-072-4. 2,126 pp., 3 Vols. . . . . **.$75.00**

INSCRIPTIONES GRAECAE AEGYPTI

Vol. I. INSCRIPTIONES NUNC CAIRO IN MUSEO
    Catalogue General des Antiquites Egyptiennes du Musee du
    Caire: Nos. 9201-9400, 26001-26123, 33001-33037. Greek
    Inscriptions. Edidit *J.G. Milne* (1905).
    ISBN 0-89005-127-5. 169 pp. **$25.00**
Vol. II. INSCRIPTIONES NUNC ALEXANDRIAE IN MUSEO
    Catalogue General des Antiquites Egyptiennes: Musee
    D'Alexandrie Nos. 1-568. Greek and Latin Inscriptions. Edidit
    E. Breccia (1911). ISBN 0-89005-242-5. xxx + 276 pp. **$25.00**
**Vol. III. INSCRIPTIONES 'MEMNONII" BESAE ORACVLI AD
ABYDVM THEBAIDIS**
    Les Graffites Grecs du Memnonion D'Abydos: Nos. 1-658.
    Ediderunt *P. Pedrizet* and *G. Lefebvre* (1919). ISBN 0-89005-
    243-3. xxv + 123 pp. **$25.00**
**Vol. IV. INSCRIPTIONES NOMINVM GRAECORVMET AEGYPTIA-
CORVM AETATIS ROMANAE, INCISAE SIVE SCRIPTAE IN
TABELLIS. "MVMMY LABELS."**
    Aegyptische und Griechische Eigennamen aus Mumieneti-
    ketten der Romischen Kaiserzeit. Edidit *W. Spiegelberg* (1901)
    ISBN 0-89005-244-1. 130 pp. + Tables. **$25.00**
Vol. V. INSCRIPTIONES CHRISTIANAE AEGYPTI.
    Recueil des Inscriptions Grecques-Chretiennes D'Egypte.
    Edidit *G. Lefebvre* (1907)
    ISBN 0-89005-248-4. xl + 176 pp. **$25.00**
    All Volumes 8½ x 11'' Hardbound and Gold-Stamped
The Set of Five Volumes **$125.00**

ORDER FORM

Author	Title	Price
	Total Books	
	THE ANCIENT WORLD $10.00 Per Four Issues	
	Postage and Handling Extra. *Minimum Charge $1.00*	
	TOTAL	

Directions For Ordering and Payment

For Fast, Economical and Convenient service order directly from: John Corvin, Order Dept./Ares Publishers Inc./612 North Michigan Ave., Suite 216/Chicago, Illinois 60611.

Personal Checks on U.S. Banks only are accepted for payment of orders. Overseas customers please pay by check in U.S. Funds drawn on an American Bank or with an International Postal Money Order. Customers anywhere in the world may charge purchases to Visa Card or Master Charge Card.

Postage and Handling Extra. *Minimum Charge $1.00*

☐ VISA [| | | | |] [| | | |] [| | | |] [| | | |] Expiry [| | | |]

☐ Master Charge [| | | | | | | | | | | | | | | | | | | | |] Expiry [| |]-[| |]
Copy number above your name on ▶ [| |]-[| |]

☐ Signature _____ on Mastercharge

NAME _____

ADDRESS _____

_____

ARES PUBLISHERS Inc.
612 NORTH MICHIGAN AVE., SUITE 216
CHICAGO, ILLINOIS 60611